The Return

The Return

Fathers, sons and the land in between

HISHAM MATAR

VIKING

an imprint of

PENGUIN BOOKS

VIKING

UK | USA | Canada | Ireland | Australia
India | New Zealand | South Africa

Viking is part of the Penguin Random House group of companies
whose addresses can be found at global.penguinrandomhouse.com.

First published 2016

001

Copyright © Hisham Matar, 2016

The moral right of the author has been asserted

Grateful acknowledgement is made for permission to quote the extract on page 189.
Copyright © Guardian News & Media Ltd, 2016

Typeset in Garamond MT Std 12.5/14.75 pt
by Palimpsest Book Production Limited, Falkirk, Stirlingshire
Printed in Great Britain by Clays Ltd, St Ives plc

A CIP catalogue record for this book is available from the British Library

Hardback ISBN: 978-0-670-92333-5
Trade Paperback ISBN: 978-0-670-92334-2

www.greenpenguin.co.uk

MIX
Paper from
responsible sources
FSC
www.fsc.org   FSC® C018179

Penguin Random House is committed to a
sustainable future for our business, our readers
and our planet. This book is made from Forest
Stewardship Council® certified paper.

Contents

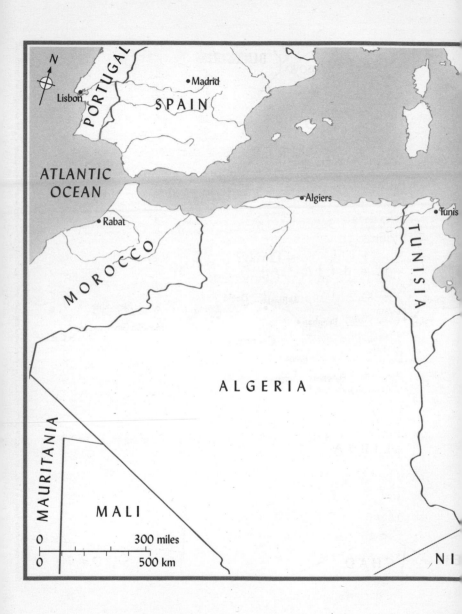

1. Trapdoor

Early morning, March 2012. My mother, my wife Diana and I were sitting in a row of seats that were bolted to the tiled floor of a lounge in Cairo International airport. Flight 835 for Benghazi, a voice announced, was due to depart on time. Every now and then, my mother glanced anxiously at me. Diana too seemed concerned. She placed a hand on my arm and smiled. I should get up and walk around, I told myself. But my body remained rigid. I had never felt more capable of stillness.

The terminal was nearly empty. There was only one man sitting opposite us. He was overweight, weary-looking, possibly in his mid fifties. There was something in the way he sat — the locked hands on the lap, the left tilt of the torso — that signalled resignation. Was he Egyptian or Libyan? Was he on a visit to the neighbouring country or going home after the revolution? Had he been for or against Qaddafi? Perhaps he was one of those undecided ones who held their reservations close to their chest?

The voice of the announcer returned. It was time to board. I found myself standing at the front of the line, Diana beside me. She had, on more than one occasion, taken me to the town where she was born in northern California. I know the plants and the colour of the light and the distances where she grew up. Now I was, finally, taking her to my land. She had packed the Hasselblad and the Leica, her two favourite cameras, and a hundred rolls of film. Diana works with great fidelity. Once she gets hold of a thread, she will follow it until the end. Knowing this excited and worried me. I am reluctant to give Libya any more than it has already taken.

Mother was pacing by the windows that looked on to the runway, speaking on her mobile phone. People – mostly men – began to fill the terminal. Diana and I were now standing at the head of a long line. It bent behind us like a river. I pretended I had forgotten something and pulled her to one side. Returning after all these years was a bad idea, I suddenly thought. My family had left in 1979, thirty-three years earlier. This was the chasm that divided the man from the eight-year-old boy I was then. The plane was going to cross that gulf. Surely such journeys were reckless. This one could rob me of a skill that I have worked hard to cultivate: how to live away from places and people I love. Joseph Brodsky was right. So were Nabokov and Conrad. They were artists who never returned. Each had tried, in his own way, to cure himself of his country. What you have left behind has dissolved. Return and you will face the absence or the defacement of what you treasured. But Dmitri Shostakovich and Boris Pasternak and Naguib Mahfouz were also right: never leave the homeland. Leave and your connections to the source will be severed. You will be like a dead trunk, hard and hollow.

What do you do when you cannot leave and cannot return?

*

Back in October 2011, I had considered never returning to Libya. I was in New York, walking up Broadway, the air cold and swift, when the proposition presented itself. It seemed immaculate, a thought my mind had manufactured independently. As in youthful moments of drunkenness, I felt bold and invincible.

I had gone to New York the previous month, at the invitation of Barnard College, to lecture on novels about exile and estrangement. But I had an older connection to the city. My parents had moved to Manhattan in the spring of 1970, when my father was appointed first secretary in the Libyan Mission to the United Nations. I was born that autumn. Three years later, in 1973, we returned to Tripoli. In the years since, I had visited New York maybe four or five times and always briefly. So, although I had just returned to the city of my birth, it was a place I hardly knew.

In the thirty-six years since we left Libya, my family and I had built associations with several surrogate cities: Nairobi, where we went on our escape from Libya, in 1979, and have continued to visit ever since; Cairo, where we settled into indefinite exile the following year; Rome, a vacation spot for us; London, where I went at the age of fifteen for my studies and where for twenty-nine years I have been doggedly trying to make a life for myself; Paris, where, fatigued and annoyed by London, I moved in my early thirties, vowing never to return to England, only to find myself back two years later. In all these cities, I had pictured myself one day calm and living in that faraway island, Manhattan, where I was born. I would imagine a new acquaintance asking me, perhaps at a dinner party, or in a café, or in changing-rooms after a long swim, that old tiresome question 'Where are you from?' and I, unfazed and free of the usual agitation, would casually reply, 'New York.' In these fantasies, I saw myself taking pleasure from the fact that such a statement would be both true and false, like a magic trick.

That I should move to Manhattan in my fortieth year, as Libya was ripping itself apart, and for this to take place on the 1st of September, the day when, back in 1969, a young captain named Muammar Qaddafi deposed King Idris and many of the significant features of my life – where I live, the language in which I write, the language I am using now to write this – were set in motion: all this made it difficult to escape the idea that there was some kind of divine will at work.

*

In any political history of Libya, the 1980s represent a particularly lurid chapter. Opponents of the regime were hanged in public squares and sports arenas. Dissidents who fled the country were pursued – some kidnapped or assassinated. The '80s were also the first time that Libya had an armed and determined resistance to the dictatorship. My father was one of the opposition's most prominent figures. The organization he belonged to had a training camp in Chad, south of the Libyan border, and several underground cells inside the country. Father's career in the army, his short tenure as a diplomat, and the private means he had managed to procure in the mid 1970s, when he became a successful businessman – importing products as diverse as Mitsubishi vehicles and Converse sports shoes to the Middle East – made him a dangerous enemy. The dictatorship had tried to buy him off; it had tried to scare him. I remember sitting beside him one afternoon in our flat in Cairo when I was ten or eleven, the weight of his arm on my shoulders. In the chair opposite sat one of the men I called 'Uncle' – men who, I somehow knew, were his allies or followers. The word 'compromise' was spoken, and Father responded, 'I won't negotiate. Not with criminals.'

Whenever we were in Europe, he carried a gun. Before getting into the car, he would ask us to stand well away. He would go down on his knees and look under the chassis, cup his hands and peek through the windows for any sign of wiring. Men like him had been shot in train stations and cafés, their cars blown up. During the 1980s, when I was still in Cairo, I had read in the newspaper about the death of a renowned Libyan economist. He was stepping off a train at Stazione Termini in Rome when a stranger pressed a pistol to his chest and pulled the trigger. The photograph printed beside the article had the figure of the deceased covered in newspaper sheets, presumably from that day's paper, which stopped at his ankles, leaving his polished leather shoes pointing up. Another time there was a report of a Libyan student shot in Greece. He was sitting on the terrace of a café in Monastiraki Square in

Athens. A scooter stopped, and the man sitting behind the driver pointed a gun at the student and fired several shots. A Libyan BBC World Service newsreader was killed in London. In April 1984, a demonstration took place in front of the Libyan embassy in St James's Square. One of the embassy staff pulled up a sash window on the first floor, held out a machine-gun and sprayed the crowd. A policewoman, Yvonne Fletcher, was killed and eleven Libyan demonstrators were wounded, some of them critically.

Qaddafi's campaign to hunt down exiled critics – which was announced by Moussa Koussa, the head of foreign intelligence, at a public rally in the early 1980s – extended to the families of dissidents. My only sibling, Ziad, was fifteen when he went off to boarding school in Switzerland. A few weeks later, midway through term, he returned to Cairo. We had all gone to collect him from the airport. When he appeared amongst those spilling out of the arrivals lounge, his face looked paler than I remembered it. A few days earlier, I had seen Mother make several telephone calls, her finger trembling as she spun the dial.

The Swiss school was remote, high up in the Alps. Public transport to the nearest village was in the form of a cable car, which operated for only a few hours in the middle of the day. For two days running, Ziad noticed a car parked on the path outside the school's main gate. It had in it four men. They had the long hair so typical of members of Qaddafi's Revolutionary Committees. Late one night, Ziad was called to the school's office telephone. On the other end of the line, a man said, 'I am a friend of your father. You must do exactly what I tell you. You have to leave immediately and take the first train to Basle.'

'Why? What happened?' Ziad asked.

'I can't tell you now. You must hurry. Take the first train to Basle. I'll be there and will explain everything.'

'But it's the middle of the night,' Ziad said.

The man would not offer any further explanations. He simply kept repeating, 'Take the first train to Basle.'

'I can't do that. I don't know who you are. Please don't call here again,' Ziad said and hung up.

The man then called Mother, who then telephoned the school. She told Ziad he needed to leave the school right away and told him what to do.

Ziad woke up his favourite teacher, a young Cambridge graduate who had probably thought it would be fun to go and teach English literature in the Alps, skiing in between classes.

'Sir, my father is about to have surgery and asked to see me before going into the operating theatre. I need to take the first train to Basle. Would you please drive me to the station?'

The teacher telephoned my mother, and she backed up Ziad's story. The headmaster had to be woken up. He telephoned Mother and, once he too was satisfied, Ziad's teacher checked the train timetable. There was a train for Basle in forty minutes. If they hurried, they might make it.

They had to drive past the car; there was no other way out. Ziad pretended to be tying his shoelace as they passed the men. The teacher drove carefully down the twisting mountain road. A few minutes later, headlights appeared

behind them. When the teacher said, 'I think they are following us,' Ziad pretended not to hear.

At the station, Ziad shot into the concourse and hid
in the public toilets. He heard the train roll in. He
waited until it had come to a complete stop, counted a
few seconds for the passengers to disembark and
board, then ran and jumped on the train. The doors
shut and the carriages moved. Ziad was sure he had
lost them, but then the four men appeared, walking up
the aisle. They saw him. One of them smiled at him.
They followed him from one carriage to the next, mut-
tering, 'Kid, you think you are a man? Then come here
and show us.' At the front of the train, Ziad found the
conductor chatting to the driver.

'Those men there are following me,' Ziad told him, no
doubt with fear rippling through his voice because the
conductor believed him at once and asked Ziad to sit right
beside him. Seeing this, the four men retreated to the next
carriage. When the train arrived, Ziad saw men in uniform
waiting on the platform. My father's associate, who had
telephoned that night, was standing amongst them.

I remember Ziad telling us these details as we sat
around the dining table. I was utterly overwhelmed by a
feeling of safety and gratitude, as well as by a new fear,
sharp and pulsing, in my depths. Looking at me, though,
you would not have known it. All the while, as Ziad spoke,
I was pretending to be excited by his adventure. It wasn't
till later that evening that the whole thing weighed down
on my consciousness. I kept thinking about what the men
had said, which Ziad whispered to us several times, per-

fectly mimicking the menacing tone and the Tripoli accent: 'Kid, you think you are a man? Then come here and show us.'

Shortly after this, when I was twelve, I needed to see an eye specialist. Mother put me on a plane and I flew alone from Cairo to Geneva, where Father was to meet me. He and I spoke on the telephone before I left for the airport.

'If, for any reason, you don't see me in arrivals, go to the information desk and ask them to call out this name,' he said, and read out one of the names he travelled on. I knew it well. 'Whatever you do,' he repeated, 'don't give them my real name.'

When I got to Geneva, I didn't see him. I did as he said and went to the information desk, but when the woman behind the counter asked me for the name, I panicked. I couldn't remember it. Seeing how flustered I was, she smiled and handed me the microphone. 'Would you like to make the announcement yourself?' I took the microphone and said 'Father, Father' several times, until I saw him running towards me, a big smile on his face. I felt embarrassed and remember asking him on the way out of the airport, 'Why couldn't I simply say your name? What are you afraid of, anyway?' We walked through the crowd, and as we did so we passed two men speaking Arabic with a perfect Libyan accent. Encountering our dialect during those years was always disconcerting, provoking in me, and with equal force, both fear and longing. 'So what does this Jaballa Matar look like, anyway?' one of them asked the other. I went silent and never complained about my father's complicated travel arrangements after that.

It was out of the question for Father to travel on his real passport. He used false documents with pseudonyms. In Egypt, we felt safe. But in March 1990, Father was kidnapped from our Cairo flat by the Egyptian secret police and delivered to Qaddafi. He was taken to Abu Salim prison, in Tripoli, which was known as 'The Last Stop' – the place where the regime sent those it wanted to forget.

In the mid 1990s, several people risked their lives to smuggle three of my father's letters to my family. In one of them, Father writes, 'The cruelty of this place far exceeds all of what we have read of the fortress prison of Bastille. The cruelty is in everything, but I remain stronger than their tactics of oppression ... My forehead does not know how to bow.'

In another letter, there is this sentence: 'At times a whole year will pass by without seeing the sun or being let out of this cell.'

In calm, precise and at times ironic prose, he demonstrates an astonishing commitment to patience:

And now a description of this noble palace ... The cell is a concrete box. The walls are made of pre-fabricated slabs. There is a steel door through which no air passes. A window that is three and a half metres above ground. As for the furniture, it is in the style of Louis XVI: an old mattress, worn out by many previous prisoners, torn in several places. The world here is empty.

From these letters, and from prisoner testimonies that I've been able to gather with the help of Amnesty International, Human Rights Watch and the Swiss NGO TRIAL, we know that Father was in Abu Salim at least from March 1990 to April 1996, when he was moved from his cell and taken to another secret wing in the same prison, moved to another prison or executed.

*

In late August 2011, Tripoli fell, and revolutionaries took control of Abu Salim. They broke down the cell doors, and eventually all the men crammed inside those concrete boxes wandered out into the sunlight. I was at home in London. I spent that day on the telephone with one of the men hammering away at the steel doors of the prison cells. 'Wait, wait,' he would shout, and I would hear his sledgehammer hitting steel. Not the sound of a bell in the open but one buried deep, like a recalled memory, ringing, *I want to be there and I don't want to be there.* Countless voices were now shouting, 'God is great!' He handed the hammer to another man, and I listened to him pant, purpose and victory in every breath. *I want to be there and I don't want to be there.* They came to a cell in the basement, the last one remaining. Lots of shouting now, people vying to lend a hand. I heard the man call out, 'What? Inside?' There was confusion. Then I heard him shout, 'Are you sure?' He got back on the phone and said they thought the cell contained an important person from Ajdabiya, my father's hometown, who had been in solitary confinement for many years. I could not speak. *I want to be there and I want to be there.* 'Stay with me,' the man on the telephone said.

Every few seconds, he would repeat, 'Stay with me.'
Whether it took ten minutes or an hour, I cannot say.
When they eventually broke down the door, they found
an old blind man in a windowless room. His skin had not
seen the sun in years. When they asked him his name, he
said he did not know. What family was he from? He did
not know. How long had he been there? He had, appar-
ently, lost his memory. He had one possession: a
photograph of my father. Why? Who was he to Father?
The prisoner did not know. And, although he could not
remember anything, he was happy to be free. That was the
word the man on the telephone used: 'happy'. I wanted to
ask about the picture. Was it a recent one or an old one?
Was it pinned to the wall, kept under the pillow, or did
they find it on the floor beside the man's bed? Was there a
bed? Did the prisoner have a bed? I asked none of these
questions. And when the man said, 'I am sorry,' I thanked
him and hung up.

*

By October, as I was attempting to concentrate on my
teaching in New York, all the political prisons, every
underground secret compartment, were falling one by
one to the revolutionaries. Cells were opened, the men in
them released and accounted for. Father was not in any of
them. For the first time, the truth became inescapable. It
was clear that he had been shot or hanged or starved or
tortured to death. No one knows when, or those who
know are dead, or have escaped, or are too frightened or

indifferent to speak. Was it in the sixth year of his incarceration, when his letters stopped? Was it in the massacre that took place that year in the same prison, when 1,270 men were rounded up and shot? Or was it a solitary death, perhaps during the seventh or the eighth or the ninth year? Or was it in the twenty-first year, after the revolution broke? Perhaps during one of the many interviews I gave, arguing the case against the dictatorship? Or perhaps Father was not dead at all, as Ziad continued to believe, even after all the prisons were opened. Perhaps, Ziad hoped, he was out and, owing to some failure – loss of memory, loss of the ability to see or speak or hear – was unable to find his way back, like Gloucester wandering the heath in *King Lear*. 'Give me your hand: you are now within a foot / Of the extreme verge,' Edgar says to his blind father, who has resolved to end his own life, a line that has lived with me these past twenty-five years.

It must have been the story of the prisoner who had lost his memory that made Ziad believe that Father might somehow be alive. A few days after I arrived in New York, Ziad called, asking me to find someone who could produce a picture of what Father might look like today so that we could post it around the country and online. 'Someone might recognize him,' he said. I spoke to a forensic artist in Canada. She wanted copies of as many photographs as possible of my father, his siblings and my grandfather. After she received them, she called with a list of questions about the conditions he endured in prison: the food he ate, the possibility of torture or illness? Ten days later, the drawing arrived. She had ruthlessly dropped the cheeks, sunk the eyes, exaggerated a faint scar on the forehead. The worst thing about the portrait was its credibility. It made me wonder about other changes. What had become of the teeth, for example, those he bared to Dr Mazzoleni in Rome on our annual check-up? The Italian dentist used to always say, provoking in us silent pride, 'You ought to be grateful to Libya and its minerals for such excellent teeth.' And what of the tongue that had its own way of shaping my name, the amplifying throat and all the parts of that echo chamber, the head – its nostrils and cavities, the weight of its bone and flesh and brain – and how it alters the resonance of that gentle voice? How would this new, older voice sound? I never sent the portrait to Ziad, and he stopped asking about it. I showed it to him the next time we were together. He looked at it for a moment and said, 'It's not accurate.' I agreed and put the drawing back in its envelope. 'Don't show it to Mother,' he added.

That cold October evening in New York, I began to doubt both my ability to return to Libya and my will not to. I entered our flat on the Upper West Side and did not tell Diana about the 'immaculate' idea that had occurred to me on my walk. We ate supper. I collected the plates and washed them slowly. Afterwards, we listened to music, then took a walk through the dark streets. I hardly slept that night. Never returning to Libya, I realized, meant never allowing myself to think about it again, which would only lead to another form of resistance, and I was done with resistance.

I left my building at daybreak. I was glad for New York's

indifference. I had always regarded Manhattan the way an orphan might think of the mother who had laid him on the doorstep of a mosque: it meant nothing to me, but also everything. It represented, in moments of desperation, the possibility of finally cheating myself out of exile. My feet were heavy. I noticed how old I had become, but also the boyishness that persisted, as if part of me had stopped developing the moment we left Libya. I was like David Malouf's imagining of Ovid in his banishment – infantilized by exile. I headed towards my office at the college. I wanted to immerse myself in work. I tried to think about the lecture I was going to deliver that afternoon, on Kafka's *The Trial*. I thought about K's tenderness towards the two men who come to execute him; his dark and heroic surrender; the words he thought to himself: 'the only thing I can do now is keep my mind calm and analytical to the last'; and the corrective, regretful discovery of: 'I've always wanted to seize the world with twenty hands …' I told myself it was good that I had the lectures to think about. I crossed over a grille in the sidewalk. Beneath it, there was a room, barely high enough for a man to stand and certainly not wide enough for him to lie down. A deep grey box in the ground. I had no idea what it was for. Without knowing how it happened, I found myself on my knees, looking in. No matter how hard I tried, I could not find a trapdoor, a pipe, anything leading out. It came over me suddenly. I wept and could hear myself.

2. Black Suit

In 1980, my family was living in Egypt. On several occasions as a child I would sit in my room with the atlas and try to calculate the number of kilometres between our flat and the border. Every year, Qaddafi was going to die or be forced to flee the country. Every year, we were going to return home. In 1985, a couple of years after Ziad's close call in Switzerland, I asked to go to boarding school in Europe. I decided on England. Because of what had happened to Ziad, I would need to use a pseudonym. We liked the music of Bob Marley and Bob Dylan, so Ziad suggested I go by the name of Bob. I was to pretend to be Christian, the son of an Egyptian mother and an American father. A year later, in 1986, I went to boarding school in England and for the following two years I lived under this identity. In the beginning, it seemed surprisingly easy. I even enjoyed pretending to be someone else.

There was a girl I liked. She had skin the colour of set honey. Her eyes were wide and gleamed like polished wood. She was a voracious reader. Every other day I saw her in the library with a different book. She had a poise that seemed mysterious to me, and a warmth that I was sure derived its strength from a stable life. I imagined how words passing through her throat might sound, but I never dared approach, and, as she was not in any of my classes, I didn't hear her voice until, at the Spring Party, she walked across the room and, to my utter surprise, asked me to dance. We danced through several songs, and then stood side by side against the wall. When it was time for us boys to be bussed back to our house, she accompanied me down the long path. The crickets in the hedge, the only light coming from a far-off lamp-post. We stopped. She placed her mouth on my cheek and left it there for a long time. I still remember the delicate temperature of her lips. I could hardly sleep from happiness. But then the following morning, when she ran over to me as I stood in line to enter the dining hall, I turned all cold and silent. I couldn't imagine kissing a mouth that had never spoken my real name. The look on her face – taken aback, betrayed – is still with me.

The year passed and I was home for the summer, eating Mother's food and hearing my name, and its various diminutive forms, spoken out loud at home and in public. I missed the Arabic language and everything Arabic: the gestures, the social code, the music. I became less boisterous as my departure date approached. My parents noticed. One afternoon Father came into my room. 'I hope you know you can always change your mind,' he said gently. But, given how hard I had lobbied to be sent abroad, I felt I must persist.

On my return to school one of my friends came to tell me about a new boy.

'He's Arabic,' he said. 'His name is Hamza.'

'Do you know where from?' I asked.

'Libya, I think – or was it Lebanon?'

I went to look up the name. It was definitely Libyan. His father worked for the government. I had no doubt that if he discovered my real family name he would recognize it. By then Father had become one of the most noted leaders of the opposition. When Hamza and I met, he extended his hand and said, 'Marhaba.' He smiled in a way that would soon become familiar. We became friends immediately. We liked similar music. On Wednesdays, when we got the afternoon off and most of the other boys went to the pub, he and I would hunt for a good restaurant. Once he told me he loved me like a brother. I said I did too.

He hardly ever talked about Libya. I hadn't seen the country for eight years. I wished I could ask him about it. Once, on a group hike through the woods, I absent-mindedly began to hum a Libyan folk song. He noticed. 'My brother's best friend is Libyan,' I said. 'Invited us to a wedding once. Crazy event. He's always bringing music tapes around. Do you know the tune? Where is it from? What are the words?'

It was at that time that my housemaster, the only person besides the headmaster who knew my true identity, began to invite me into his home. He was Welsh. He looked like Ted Hughes and, like the poet, was a keen fisherman. He always smelt of cigar. Some nights, just after lights out, he would knock on the door and whisper, 'Robert, telephone call.' I would follow him down to his flat, where he lived with his wife, their four children and two dogs. We would sit at the kitchen table. He would pour me a small glass of red wine and his wife would fry me an egg. He never called me by my real name. He simply afforded me the chance every now and then to be who I really was.

That special thing, when a friendship comes to resemble a shelter, began to occur between Hamza and me. When the year ended and we were to go our separate ways, I wondered how our bond, hermetically sealed within the school, could ever survive. I was secretly relieved when he got a place at Cardiff University; I was going to university in London. For the farewell, Hamza and I met with a group of other students at a pub in the nearby village. It was an exuberant night, full of promises that we would stay in touch forever. More than once I would look at their faces and hear the word 'impossible' ringing in my head. How could I ever see these people again, even the dearest one amongst them? I decided to leave. I went to use the toilet before heading off to the station. Hamza followed me. I remember our parallel images in the mirror as we stood washing hands. We embraced. 'Man,' he said, 'I'm going to miss you.' I remember the shape of his ear, how my eyes focused on it. I said the words as though involuntarily:

'Hamza, I am Libyan. My name is Hisham Matar. I'm the son of Jaballa Matar.'

He didn't let go. I felt his body become rigid.

'I am sorry,' I said. I was not sure what exactly I was apologizing for.

When we looked at each other we had tears running down our faces. We embraced again, rushed back to the bar and continued drinking. We all stayed there until the place closed. Neither of us mentioned a word to the others. He never called me Hisham.

He insisted, swearing on his father's life, on paying for a cab to take me all the way to London. Midway through the journey I had to ask the driver to pull over. I vomited on the side of the motorway.

Years later, walking with Diana up the Marylebone Road, I saw him coming in the opposite direction. He had clearly spotted me first, because that same smile was drawn on his face. We shook hands and embraced. I introduced him to Diana. And he had that proud shyness intimate friends feel on first meeting your beloved. We searched our pockets for pieces of paper. We wrote our telephone numbers down. But, even as we did, I was sure that we both knew that neither of us would ever call.

*

I am still not entirely clear why my fifteen-year-old self, living inside a loving, unrestrictive family, would choose to leave Egypt, the horses, the Red and Mediterranean seas, the friends, Thunder – the German Shepherd I fed with my own hands (and who was anything but thunderous) – and, perhaps most importantly, my own name, and fly 3,500 kilometres north to live in a large, unheated stone house with forty English boys in the middle of soggy fields and under a sky that almost never broke, where I was Robert and only sometimes Bob.

I had fallen for the landscape some five years before, when I was ten. We were visiting London, but then, hear-

ing that a cousin was boarding in a school in Somerset
– or was it Dorset or perhaps even Devon? – we decided
to take the train west from Paddington. I remember the
station, and the way the carriage seemed to become lighter
as the density of the capital fell away, as though the pull
of gravity was stronger in the city. It was impossible to
stop looking out of the window. The thick green hedge-
rows, now coming closer, now vanishing. Water running
in rivers, or lingering in drops on leaves, making the air
sharp and damp. Once we were off the train, we drove
through hedges that rose high on either side of the road.
The further we went, the narrower and deeper the lanes
became, as if the earth were folding us in. The light did
not alter. The variation was only in the clouds, interlaced
thickly together, their bellies pale and their edges a shade
darker. It all gave me the impression, which I see now was
a strange thing for a ten-year-old boy to think, that if I
were to put something down here, something of personal
value that might be, to anyone else, of no value at all and
therefore more vulnerable to damage, it would not be
moved. I would be able to come back later and find it
exactly where I had left it.

This, however, could only partly account for the odd
decision to go to English boarding school. After all, I had
a choice. I could have gone to Switzerland, a country that
has always appealed to me, or to America, which then
seemed the most exciting place in the world. But I think I
had spotted, even then, from that first visit when I was
ten, a correspondence with this strange place. Over the
years, that correspondence gained such depth that now I

feel bound to England not so much by the length of time I have spent here but by nature.

If this explains my coming to England, it does not explain my departure from Cairo. Perhaps I did not trust in the constancy of my parents' life, or the life they had created for themselves in Egypt, where many decisions were suspended because 'We'll be in Libya by then.' It's not that England felt more permanent but that here I thought I could be in charge of my own fate.

However, this love affair with the English landscape turned dark on my first day. The instructions from my parents were that, on landing at Heathrow, I was to take a black London cab directly to school. What my parents thought would be a comfort turned into a stressful journey. The London driver got lost. Night was falling. The man became more and more impatient. He threatened to leave my giant suitcase and me in one of the deserted country lanes.

Looking back, I think I might have annoyed him earlier. He had stopped at a petrol station to refuel and left the engine running. Coming from Cairo, where drivers turn off the ignition at traffic stops, this seemed horribly wasteful. My upbringing placed a heavy moral value on waste. A few grains of rice left on my plate would provoke my mother to say, 'But how precisely have these grains offended you now?' When the London cabby got back into the car, I asked him, 'Excuse me, please, why didn't you switch off your engine?' He looked at me in the rear-view mirror and said, 'You're right there, mate; it's *my* engine.' After about an hour more of driving around in the dusk, he stopped the car and asked me to get out. I decided to remain silent. Exasperated, he swung the car arbitrarily into the next lane, and, as the road rose, I spotted two horseback-riders some fifty metres away.

'Stop,' I said, and proceeded to wave desperately to the riders, shouting, 'Hello! Hello!'

They saw me. Two women. I was later to learn that they were the local farmer's daughters and that they almost never rode this late, but, as luck had it, they were looking for their dog, which had gone missing that afternoon. They looked slightly older than Ziad and me, but the age difference between them seemed similar. They remained on their horses: a mare and stallion, each taller than the cab, coats brushed, glistening.

In Cairo, between the ages of eleven and fifteen, I used to rise at 5 a.m. each morning to ride before school. And on the nights I went out with the boys and our gallivanting lasted until we heard the call for dawn prayer, we would head out to the stables behind the Giza Pyramids and ride out into the desert. When the horses were warm and the sun had appeared above the horizon, we would gallop the whole way back. I would bring my face as close as possible to the mane, against the warmth of the animal's neck, listening to its breath racing in and out as though through a piston. The stable boy would rub his hand on the horses and show us the sweat's white foam, shouting that we had ruined the animals for the rest of the day. We would pay him double and, if he was still cross, bring him with us to the Mena House Oberoi for breakfast.

These English horses were at least double the size of those we rode in Cairo, bred for winter farm work and hunting rather than racing. The sisters knew of the school. The older one pointed out a building in the distance, then told the driver, in a commanding voice that secretly pleased me, 'Well, you won't see it from down there now, will you?' He stepped out and saw the dark stone tower jutting out of a clump of high trees, their leaves already discolouring. As the older sister gave the driver directions, the younger one sat perfectly still and looked at me. She had red hands, sore from riding in the cold evening, and the difference in colour between her dark fingers and pale pink face seemed so strange to me then.

*

Four days before Mother, Diana and I were due to go to Benghazi, I flew from London to Cairo. On the way, an old question resolved itself. It suddenly made sense why my friends have always assumed that, after more than a quarter of a century of living in England, I will eventually move to another country. Something about me, or about the life I have created in London, seems impermanent. This suspicion, that at any moment I might leave, has disturbed but also reassured me. I am often unnerved by exiles I meet who, like me, have found themselves living in London but who, unlike me, have surrendered to the place and therefore exude the sort of resigned stability I lack. Naked adoption of native mannerisms or the local dialect – this has always seemed to me a kind of humiliation. And yet, like a jealous lover, I believed I knew London's secrets better than most of its natives. When, after Prime Minister Tony Blair's visit to Libya in 2004, members of Qaddafi's inner circle began to buy houses in the British capital, sometimes in my neighbourhood, I told myself that my London was not theirs. I became grateful to have settled in a city whose most essential character is secrecy. On the plane from London to Cairo, I understood the logic of these contradictions; they were informed not by London but by the condition of waiting. It turns out that I have spent all the time since I was eight years old, when my family left Libya, waiting. My silent condemnation of those fellow-exiles who wished to assimilate – which is to say, my bloody-minded commitment to rootlessness – was my feeble act of fidelity to the old country, or maybe not even to Libya but to the young boy I was when we left.

I remained standing to one side of the line in the Cairo airport, pretending that I had lost or suddenly remembered something. I was secretly longing for our London flat. I could see its kitchen worktop unattended, the view from the rear windows, the grey stillness of the twilight, the furniture, our pictures, the rows of books. We should spend a few days in Cairo, then return to London. I had the number for Mustafa, the driver Diana and I have when we are in Cairo. He could not be that far from the airport. In a few hours, we could all be gathered around Mother's dining table for lunch. And perhaps one day we might even laugh as we recalled the day we came dangerously close to returning to Libya.

I wondered why I had worn a black suit, a suit I had bought a year before, when I was, for a fleeting moment, persuaded that there was something monastic and peaceful about a life spent in black suits. I had worn it only twice since buying it and on both occasions felt uncomfortable with how badly the cut fitted me and with the knowledge of the exorbitant amount I had spent on it. And now, for some reason, I was travelling home in this ill-fitting suit. I had got up very early that morning. I had put on a white shirt and the black suit, and taken a few moments to choose a tie, knotted it around my neck, then taken it off and hung it in the wardrobe, the same wardrobe that had been mine when I was a boy, because the room in Cairo where Diana and I slept the night before we flew to Libya, lying on our sides to fit on the narrow mattress, was my old room. I was now fifteen. I was now forty-one. I was now eight.

At the airport, my mother was still by the windows, talking on the telephone to Ziad. This was the third time he had called that morning. The three of us – Ziad, Mother and I – had planned to return to Libya together, since (and this was not mentioned but understood) we could never go back together, not completely, because Father was no longer with us. Ziad had not been able to wait. He had gone to Libya nine months earlier, in June 2011, when the war was still raging. I remember the day he telephoned to say that he was 200 kilometres from the

Libyan border. Diana and I were in a remote part of southern France, where I was writing an introduction to Turgenev's *On the Eve*. Ziad's voice kept breaking up. I drove up the hill to try to get a better signal. In the past, whenever he considered returning, he would call me, and I managed to dissuade him. This time, he did not dial my number until he had driven for six hours: first north towards Alexandria, then west, following the coastal road to the Egyptian–Libyan border. He did not want to discuss it; he just wanted me to know. We were disconnected. Every time I tried, his line was engaged. Everyone, I imagined – relatives, friends and even acquaintances – was calling to wish him well.

I had spent that morning, while Ziad was bidding his wife and four children farewell, thinking about the actions of a fictitious man, Andrei Bersyenev, in *On the Eve*. There was a detail about him that I had overlooked on previous readings: a 'vague, unfathomable emotion lurked secretly in his heart; he was sad with a sadness that had nothing noble in it. This sadness did not prevent him, however, from setting to work on the *History of the Hohenstaufen*, and beginning to read it at the very page at which he had left off the evening before.' Bersyenev is a Russian student of philosophy who concerns himself, on the eve of the Crimean War, with a German monarchic dynasty from the High Middle Ages; that is perhaps as absurd as a Libyan novelist, during the bloody days of the 17th of February Revolution, sitting in a small cabin in France, trying to write a couple of thousand words about a Russian novel published a century and a half earlier.

In the few seconds we talked, I heard in Ziad's voice that resolute tone he uses when he is about to tell me something he thinks I may object to. It would have been pointless to warn him of the danger, to remind him of the promise we had made to return together. So, when I got through to him again, I told him how wonderful it was that he was finally going home. He said he would call as soon as he was inside the country.

Later that day, Diana took me to the Plage des Brouis, a beach she had discovered along the coast on the way to Cap Lardier. We climbed up into the rocky reserve. We entered the unexpected silence trees create by the sea. The changed light. The moistness in the air becoming slightly more material. The trail was often too narrow to allow us to walk side by side. It was comforting to walk behind her. There were tall pines and eucalypti. There were wild flowers and occasionally a butterfly. The path curved and descended. Sometimes we were right by the water, close enough to touch it, and at other moments we climbed so high we were looking down at the sea from a great height. We often stopped and glanced at the view. I had my mobile phone in the pocket of my swimming trunks. Since the revolution, I had had it near me at all times: on the kitchen worktop when I was cooking, on the tiled floor when I was taking a bath. We had walked out so far that there was no signal now. I suggested we turn back, but Diana wanted to keep going. We were more than half-way to the cove. Anxiety is a shameful business. I followed her, but I was silent and impatient. When we arrived at the Plage des Brouis, my telephone caught a signal. I had a voicemail from Mother. Ziad had arrived. He had a local SIM card. She read out the number. I did not have a pen. I listened to the message again and drew the digits in the sand with my foot, large enough for a small plane flying by to see them. Diana was looking up, towards one end of the cove, where three seagulls floated in mid-air. They held their wings out and every so often would bend them to drop a metre or two, as if pretending to fall, as if playing dead, then glide up again and repeat the manoeuvre. The activity seemed to have no clear motive. Perhaps it was for the pleasure of it. Perhaps this was a spot they returned to, knowing how the arch of the cove traps the wind. Ziad answered after the first ring. He called me by my old nickname and then laughed. I laughed too.

That was his first time back. He went again after Tripoli fell, in August, and Mother went with him. I was the last, the youngest and the last, just as when I was a boy and was told to always fill the glasses of my parents and older brother before my own.

3. The Sea

On the 1st of September 1969, fourteen months before I was born, an event took place that was to change the course of Libyan history and my life. In my mind's eye, I see a Libyan army officer crossing St James's Square at about 2 p.m. towards what was then the Libyan embassy in London. He had gone to the British capital on official business. He was popular amongst his peers, although his gentle reserve was sometimes mistaken for arrogance. He had committed to memory pages of verse that, many years later when he was imprisoned, would become his comfort and companion. Several political prisoners told me that, at night, when the prison fell silent, when, in Uncle Mahmoud's words, 'You could hear a pin drop or a grown man weep softly to himself,' they heard this man's voice, steady and passionate, reciting poems. 'He never ran out of them,' his nephew, who was in prison at the same time, told me. And I remember this man who never ran out of poems telling me once that 'knowing a book by heart is like carrying a house inside your chest.'

It was a routine visit to the embassy, perhaps to collect the post or to file a report on the progress of his mission. I imagine him taking off his cap as he entered the building. The corridors were busy with clerks running here and there. Others gathered around a radio. A 27-year-old captain no one had heard of had marched on Tripoli and assumed power. My father ran out of the embassy and hailed a cab for the airport.

That is what I remember him saying the first time he told me the story. We were in London; Ziad and I were at university by then, and Father was passing through town. We had cooked him a meal in the small flat we shared. We all ate too much and either went to Regent's Park, my father walking between us, or retired to the room next door and lay on the two single beds, talking. I cannot remember clearly. If we had been in the park, then it was one of those long summer afternoons when the light remains unchanging for hours, as if the sun has stopped moving; and, if in the bedroom, then talking in low voices, sleepy but still missing each other too much to nap. Either way, I remember him saying that he had run out of the embassy and hailed a cab. But St James's Square is not known for traffic. He probably waited in front of the embassy for a few seconds and then circled around the green before walking (I picture him walking, not running) into one of the neighbouring streets. He did not know London well. He might not have gone east to Regent Street or south to Pall Mall. Had I been with him, I would have known exactly which way to go. He took the taxi directly to Heathrow and found a seat on the first flight to Tripoli.

In Cairo, shortly before he was kidnapped, Father retold the story, adding a new detail. When he entered the embassy and heard that a coup d'état had taken place, he jumped on to the reception desk in the lobby and took down the picture of the monarch he had served and admired. It was only then that I understood that it was not out of concern alone that my father rushed home on hearing of the overthrow of King Idris but also out of enthusiasm for a modern republican age. I understood then why I had always found something melancholy about an old newspaper cutting showing a portrait of King Idris jammed between the frame and the mirror of the chiffonier in my parents' bedroom. No one spoke about it, and no one removed it. It stood fading during the years of my childhood.

When my father was on that flight home from London, Libya's new ruler, Muammar Qaddafi, promoted himself from captain to colonel and issued orders that senior military officers be arrested. My father was taken straight from the Tripoli airport to prison. Five months later, he was released and stripped of his rank and uniform. He returned to his wife and three-year-old son, Ziad. The new regime then did with my father what it did with most officers who were high ranking under Idris. Not wanting to make enemies of senior military men, yet at the same time fearing their potential disloyalty, it sent them abroad, often as minor diplomats. This allowed time for the new security apparatus to form. My father was given an administrative role in Libya's Mission to the United Nations soon after his release. I was conceived in that short window of time between my father's release and his departure for New York: a time of uncertainty, but also a time of optimism, because, as his retelling of the embassy story suggested, Father had high hopes for the new regime.

Maybe he saw his imprisonment, removal from the army and temporary banishment as natural repercussions – perhaps even reversible – of the country's historical transformation. He, like many of his generation, was inspired by the example of Egypt, where, led by Gamal Abdel Nasser, a young, secular and nationalist pan-Arab republic replaced a corrupt monarchy. Qaddafi had declared his admiration for Nasser, and Nasser gave his full support to Qaddafi. So, as reluctant as my father must have been to leave Libya, I don't imagine he went to New York in despair. It took a couple of years – after Qaddafi abrogated all existing laws and declared himself de facto leader forever – for Father to discover the true nature of the new regime.

Even he, with his intolerance for superstition, must have sensed an ill omen in an event that took place on his first day at work in New York. Crossing First Avenue towards the UN building, my father saw a lorry collide with a cyclist. The limbs of the cyclist were scattered across the asphalt. My father's response was to collect the pieces of flesh and bone and respectfully place them beside the torso, which, like the twisted bicycle, had landed on the pavement. I have always associated the irrevocable and violent changes my family and my country went through in the following four decades with the image of my father – a poet turned officer turned, reluctantly, diplomat – dressed in a suit and tie, far away from home, collecting the pieces of a dead man. He was thirty-one years old. I was born later that year.

In 1973, before I turned three, my father handed in his

resignation from his UN job. He said that he and his wife missed home and wanted their two sons to grow up in Libya. This was true but certainly not the whole story, and I suspect the regime knew it. Surely his objections to government intrusion into civic society, the deliberate ways in which Qaddafi compromised the independence of the judiciary and the freedom of the press, had been noted. He had voiced them at public social gatherings. From this point on, my father had the attention of the dictatorship. It was said that even the way he walked irritated the authorities. It exuded defiance. When I first heard this, I thought, how perceptive it was. Even as a young child, I could never imagine my father bowing, and even then I wanted to protect him. He has always seemed to me the quintessence of what it means to be independent. This, together with his unresolved fate, has complicated my own independence. We need a father to rage against. When a father is neither dead nor alive, when he is a ghost, the will is impotent. I am the son of an unusual man, perhaps even a great man. And when, like most children, I rebelled against these early perceptions of him, I did so because I feared the consequences of his convictions; I was desperate to divert him from his path. It was my first lesson in the limits of one's ability to dissuade another from a perilous course. My ambitions, when it came to my father, were ordinary. Like that famous son in *The Odyssey* – like most sons, I suspect – I wished that 'at least I had some happy man / as father, growing old in his own house'. But, unlike Telemachus, I continue, after twenty-five years, to endure my father's 'unknown death and silence'. I envy the finality of funerals. I covet the certainty. How it must be to wrap one's hands around the bones, to choose how to place them, to be able to pat the patch of earth and sing a prayer.

*

In the '70s, we lived in central Tripoli, a short distance from my maternal grandfather's house. I remember the high eucalyptus trees in the front garden, their big and vivid shadows on the ground, black claws on the cars. If there was a breeze, shade and light moved. Ziad and I played football on the paved part to the side of the house, where I watched for the first time a sheep being slaughtered. It was alive, and then suddenly it was not. The animal kicked furiously, snorting for air, which entered its nostrils and escaped through the open neck. The blood poured out black and thick like date syrup. Small translucent bubbles grew and burst around its mouth. I snapped my fingers, I clapped my hands beside its wide-open eye. When it did not respond, I began to cry. I went back when the corpse was headless, skinned and hanging from a pole. The layer of fat around the body was as thin and luminous as a veil of clouds at dusk. Moments later, I sat around the table with the others and ate liver and kidneys sautéed with chilli, onion, garlic, parsley and coriander, and agreed that the dish did taste better than at any other time because the meat was, as one of the adults had said, 'unbelievably fresh'.

A few years later, we moved near El-Medina el-Seyahiya

club, on the western fringe of Tripoli. A new house. The smell of fresh paint. The vacant atmosphere of rooms where no one had ever slept before. A barren garden. My mother planted rosebushes in the front, a new baby vine in the back. Every year, it fruited grapes as small as pearls. If you ate them a week or two after they had become ripe, the sugar burnt in your throat. We planted lemon and orange trees. Those were some of the most tumultuous years in the Qaddafi era. Revolutionary Committees were set up to punish dissent. They monitored every aspect of life. Critics of the dictatorship were executed. The Committees hanged students in front of Benghazi cathedral and from the gates of the universities. Traffic was diverted to ensure that commuters saw the dangling corpses. Books and musical instruments that were deemed 'anti-revolutionary' or 'imperialist' were confiscated from shops, schools and homes, piled high in public squares and set alight. Intellectuals, businessmen, union organizers and students were shown on television, sitting handcuffed on the floor, dictating confessions to the camera.

One of the ways that my parents tried to shield Ziad and me from the madness that was unravelling outside our home was by making sure that every minute of our day was filled. We went to school, returned just in time for piano lessons, had lunch, then were off to El-Medina el-Seyahiya club for swimming. We would spend the rest of the day by the sea; the sea was our territory. There were a few adults around, but they were so eccentric that they seemed part of our imagination. There was an old man with milky eyes who sat all day by the harbour, fishing. None of us ever saw him catch anything. Then there was El-Hindi, a Native American who had somehow ended up in Tripoli. One story was that he had run away because he had killed a white man back in America. Another was that on his travels around the world he had stopped in Tripoli and was so struck by our city's beauty that he decided to never leave. Sometimes the two stories were interlaced. He used to stand on the bridge by the harbour and dive with his arms outstretched, bringing them together only before entering the water. We would all line up to watch. My idea of swimming then was to front crawl until I could no longer see land. I would float in the deep waters and then spin myself around until I lost direction.

*

That day in June, in southern France, the day Ziad entered Libya, I swam out alone into the same Mediterranean Sea. For some reason, I remembered, more vividly than ever before, that it was my father who had taught me how to swim: holding me up, one open hand against my belly, saying, 'That's it.' I never feared the sea until he was gone.

4. The Land

The plane was full. We sat down, but then Mother got up to let me sit beside the window. 'To see your country,' she said. The plane door was shut. I took out my journal and began writing, slowly and deliberately. The panic, like the dreams in which I open my mouth and nothing comes out, was born of loss. Or that recurring dream I used to have after they took my father, in which I found I had drifted deep out to sea. All four horizons are water, and the feeling is not only of fear but also of a sort of vertigo of regret. The words I was trying to write, the notebook and pen, the aeroplane, the view of the runway outside my window, my companions – the woman who bore me and the woman beside whom I matured into a man – seemed theoretical propositions.

Back in the terminal, Mother, no doubt detecting my anxiety, had asked a mischievous question. 'Who's returning?' she said. 'Suleiman el-Dewani or Nuri el-Alfi?' Suleiman el-Dewani and Nuri el-Alfi are the exiled protagonists of my novels *In the Country of Men* and *Anatomy of a Disappearance*, respectively. She wanted to cheer me up, but also implicit in her question was a warning against what she knew I was intent on doing: searching for my father. She had seen, in the years since we lost Father, how I had changed. My initial shock and silence turned to

anger, then hot activism, which determined a routine, cul-
minating in managing a campaign that consumed me for
the two years that preceded the revolution. Through it all,
Mother worried. I have long suspected that her anxieties
were not only about the dangers my search for my father
was exposing me to, or indeed what it might lead me to
uncover, but about something else far more specific, concerning the daily restlessness such a search demands,
the way it reverberates through your body and days and
everything you do. She knew that my will to find out what
happened had turned into an obsession. And when we
were sitting in the airport terminal, what her question,
spoken in a tone that was perfectly balanced between
seriousness and jest, was really saying was that she would
much rather I return with my two fictional characters than
be carrying the ghost of my father, the man she calls the
Absent-Present.

For months after we left Libya, when I was a child, I
used to lie staring at the ceiling, imagining my return. I
pictured how I would kiss the ground; take charge once
again of my chariot, that bicycle I fussed over and oiled
every week; embrace my cousins. Now they were all grown
men and women with children. Our escape from Libya
had been in stages. First, in 1979, it was Mother, Ziad and
I. A year later, Father travelled south by land through the
vast Libyan Desert and crossed the porous border into
Chad. He made his way to the capital, N'Djamena, and
boarded a plane for Rome. My parents' main bank account
was there. Free of the risk that the lines might be tapped,
he and my mother were like new lovers, spending hours

on the telephone from Rome to Cairo. Perhaps those conversations were not only attempting to resolve the two preoccupations of every exile: longing and logistics. Maybe he had had second thoughts; perhaps she, however determined, had suddenly perceived the reality of living away from home. He purchased some of the things he wanted for this new life: hand-painted china, feather pillows, silver candelabras. The consolation of fine objects. Once he joined us in Cairo, we moved to a bigger and better flat. It was there that I understood that we were not going back, that I had been tricked. I demanded to be returned to my country. My mother tried to console me. 'Leave him be,' Father told her. 'He'll get used to it.' It was the cruellest thing he had ever said. Cruel and nearly true. Even then I knew, more from the voice than from the words, and also from the way he stood, not facing me, that he too was mourning the loss. There is a moment when you realize that you and your parent are not the same person, and it usually occurs when you are both consumed by a similar passion.

There it was, the land. Rust and yellow. The colour of newly healed skin. Perhaps I will finally be released. The land got darker. Green sprouting, thinly covering hills. And, suddenly, my childhood sea. How often exiles romanticize the landscape of the homeland. I have cautioned myself against that. Nothing used to irritate me more than a Libyan waxing lyrical about 'our sea', 'our land', 'the breeze of the homeland'. Privately, though, I continued to believe that the light back home was unmatched. I continued to think of every sea, no matter how beautiful, as an impostor. Now, catching these first glimpses of the country, I thought that, if anything, it was more luminous than I remembered. The fact that it had existed all this time, that it remained as it was all these years, that I was able to recognize it, felt like an exchange, a call and its echo, a mutual expression of recognition.

We landed. I wrote the time and the date: 10.45 a.m., the 15th of March 2012. Only then did it occur to me that, after all the attempts to synchronize our schedules, the date that Diana, Mother and I had settled on, which, invariably, felt accidental, marked the twenty-second anniversary of my father's first week in captivity. He had written to us about waking up on the floor of an Abu Salim prison cell, his hands tied behind his back, his eyes blindfolded. He could hear, a few doors down, the voice of the then deputy head of the Egyptian secret service:

> Colonel Mohamed Abdel Salam [el-Mahgoub], who was the man who orchestrated the whole thing, had preceded us to Libya. It was a dirty deal. The Egyptian regime sold itself and its conscience. The deal was in the full knowledge of President Hosni Mubarak.

Looking out of the aeroplane window, I wondered if they had taken the blindfold off once Father was inside the plane. Did they allow him at least a chance to see the land from the air? Years later, I met a man who claimed to have met another man who worked on the runway in Tripoli and recalled seeing a private jet land and a man being escorted from it. The date and the time matched. The description of the prisoner suggested that he might have been my father. 'His hair was completely white. Well dressed. Handcuffed and blindfolded. A proud gait.' This was the land my father loved more than anything else. 'Don't put yourselves in competition with Libya. You will always lose,' he had said, when once the three of us had tried to dissuade him from openly opposing Qaddafi. The silence that followed was the distance between him and us. The disagreement had a historical dimension. It placed a nation against the intimate reality of a family. I looked at the wild flowers beside the runway. Spring in full bloom. And, when we stepped out of the aeroplane, the familiar scents in the air were like a blanket you were not aware you needed, but now that it has been placed on your shoulders you are grateful. My childhood friend, cousin Marwan al-Tashani, a Benghazi judge, stood at the foot of the ladder, smiling, holding a camera.

5. Blo'thaah

The deeper we drove into Benghazi, the more material the world became. We went to Marwan's house, where we found a large family gathering waiting for us. After lunch, I slipped away on a walk. I felt strong and oddly detached, separate, not what we say sometimes on recounting dreams, 'watching myself from the outside', but so involved that it seemed pointless to be anxious any more.

We checked into our hotel just as the sun was setting. Diana and I in one room, Mother next door, both rooms with windows looking out on to the sea. We were on the fourth floor. The square frame of our window was half sea, half sky. The telephone kept ringing. I have only one sibling but 130 first cousins. This meant that there were hundreds of people to see. But I had made up my mind before leaving London that my first visit would be to Uncle Mahmoud and my aunts – my father's siblings – in nearby Ajdabiya, the city where my father grew up. The following morning, we set off on the two-hour drive south.

Uncle Mahmoud is my father's youngest brother. My father was born in 1939, Mahmoud in 1955. In old photographs, Father is serious and poised, well groomed even in his youth; Uncle Mahmoud has the long hair of the 1960s and '70s, a smile always lurking. Father was born into a Libya ruled by Benito Mussolini. He was four in 1943, when the Italo-German armies were defeated in North Africa and Libya fell to the British and the French. On the 24th of December 1951, when, under King Idris, Libya gained its independence, Father was twelve years old. Uncle Mahmoud was born four years later. In 1969, the year of Qaddafi's coup, Father was thirty, and Uncle Mahmoud fourteen. Mahmoud seemed both uncle and brother to Ziad and me, a rare ally with an insider's knowledge of adulthood. When Father resigned from the diplomatic corps in New York and we moved back to Tripoli, Uncle Mahmoud came and stayed with us. He loved Voltaire and Russian novels. He had a dreamy sensibility and would often forget to turn the stove off. Unlike all the other adults, he never turned down my appeals to go out to the garden, even after lunch, when the sun was merciless and the household napped. We played football or sat in the shade of the eucalyptus trees. I knew that his love for me was uncomplicated and unequivocal, and knowing this felt like a great freedom. In our exile years, Father would often tell me that I reminded him of his little brother.

In the same week in March 1990 that my father was kidnapped, Libyan secret service agents drove to Uncle Mahmoud's home in Ajdabiya. Other officials went to Hmad Khanfore, my uncle through marriage, and to my paternal aunt's sons, cousins Ali and Saleh Eshnayquet. All four men were arrested. They belonged to one of the underground cells that my father's organization had set up inside the country. The arrests were so well coordinated that every man captured believed the others were still free. Each assumed that he was the only one being interrogated and tortured. In January 2011, as the Tunisian and Egyptian revolutions unfolded, the Libyan dictatorship grew anxious. Wanting to appease popular discontent, it let out some political prisoners. I became hopeful. The public campaign for the release of my father and relatives, which I had started a couple of years earlier, went into full gear. On the 3rd of February of that year, and after twenty-one years of imprisonment, all except for my father were set free. Fourteen days later, bolstered by the successful overthrows of the Tunisian and Egyptian dictators, a popular uprising exploded across Libya.

I had spoken to Uncle Mahmoud on the telephone from London moments after he was released. He was in a car, being driven home. He did not talk about the role I might have played in gaining his liberty, but nonetheless I could sense his gratitude, and it made me feel uneasy. He asked if I knew of a certain Libyan poet living in Dublin: 'You should look him up, he mentions you in an article. And do you recall giving an interview to the Arabic BBC?' It was one of the first interviews I gave on the publication of my first novel, and I remembered how I thought that, if my father was alive, he might hear it. 'I put the radio next to my ear and heard every word,' Uncle Mahmoud said. Then he proceeded to quote to me, with extraordinary accuracy, some of the questions the interviewer had asked and my responses. And, for the following few minutes, everything he said began with 'Do you remember ...', listing memories, my childhood idiosyncrasies, the things we used to do together. Then, just before we hung up, he said, 'Don't lose hope.'

*

Preparing for the trip, I had vowed that, in the search for my father, I would take everything I had learnt about intuition, instinct and sensitivity and apply it as sharply as I could. I would keep myself available to what places might tell me about what had happened to him. One location that Diana and I had intended to visit in Tripoli was Abu Salim prison, where Father had been held. I imagined us walking across its infamous courtyard, where so much blood had been spilled, and into its long corridors lined with the doors that the revolutionaries had hammered open. But the closer the date of our trip approached, the less possible it seemed that I would be able to visit the prison. I knew that Diana wanted to photograph it. I could imagine those yet to be captured pictures in my mind. But even before we landed in Libya I found myself telling her that under no circumstances were we to go to Abu Salim. I cannot think of any other instance when I forbade my wife from doing anything. I could not bear the thought of someone I love being in that place; that was the reason I gave Diana. The truth was that I lacked the strength to go to Abu Salim. I worried that if I found myself in those cells I had heard about, imagined, dreamt about for years – dark places where I had several times wanted to be, so as to finally be reunited with my father – that if I found myself in that place where his smell, and times, and spirit lingered (for they must linger), I might be forever undone.

When I think of what might have happened to him, I feel an abyss open up beneath me. I am clutching at the walls. They are rough and unreliable, made of soft clay that flakes off in the rain. The pit is circular. Like a well. Our well. For, although my family has been in Ajdabiya for generations, there is another place, about thirty kilometres deeper into the desert, which is our older and more private home. Until my grandfather died, the family used to decamp there every year for the spring months, and live in tents. Now it is where the family keeps its camels and where my cousins often go to picnic. Two ancient Greek reservoirs carved deep into the belly of the desert, collecting the scarce rainwater. Its name, whose meaning and linguistic origin we do not know, is Blo'thaah. My father was born there, in the spring of 1939.

The abyss opens too when I think why I never searched, when I was in Libya, for the men who knew Father in prison, particularly the man Ziad met on his return to Libya in 2011, and who had claimed to have been in the cell next door to Father's back in the mid 1990s. Neighbours. How often have I gone over his account – the account he gave Ziad – in my head or out loud to Diana. Yet the fear is there too when I think of finding this man, of doing what seems to be the loyal thing to do, the sensible thing to do, to hear from him all the things he had told Ziad about what life was like for Father in prison, to ask the questions Ziad might have missed, because I have always been known in my family for being good with details. 'What time is your flight?' was my response to Father's dramatic announcement in London, a few months before he was kidnapped, that he was going to his organization's military camp in Chad, that it was time for him and his men to cross the border into Libya and finally act. They planned to make their way north to the capital and, with the help of associates in several Libyan towns and cities, strike at key locations and overthrow the regime. He did not tell us any of this. All he said was that he was going to Chad and might never return, and that he wanted us to take care of our mother, to take care of ourselves, live as honest men. This was shortly after his father died, and I saw in his eyes that he was more determined than ever. 'What time is your flight?' I had asked, refusing to turn down the volume on the TV, which was showing an opera, Pavarotti with his mouth wide open. Ziad was crying. I refused to cry.

*

The road to Ajdabiya had always been desolate, but this year the rains had been heavy, and the desert on both sides of the highway was dotted with wild green shrubbery. Small trees leant in the direction of the wind. Every now and then, we passed tanks and military trucks, hollowed out and rusting in the sun. At one point, we stopped the car and walked over to one of the tanks. The steel curled brown-red like a giant autumn leaf. On the 18th of March 2011, a loyalist armoured column marched from Ajdabiya towards Benghazi. Qaddafi meant to punish the city, make an example of it, and put an end to the revolt. According to several accounts, some of these trucks and tanks were packed with green flags and placards that read: BENGHAZI USED TO BE HERE.

At every major junction, a thick rope was stretched across the highway. Young men stood carrying rifles. They peered into the car and waved us on. They wore fatigues, and, although they received funds from the fledgling Tripoli government, they were not under its authority. Every checkpoint was under the command of a 'revolutionary', who would distribute the salaries. There were countless claims of embezzlement. But these bands, I was told, were small fish. Larger militias controlled oil fields, ports and public buildings. A member of the National Transitional Council, the de facto government, told me that, because a national army and police force did not yet exist, the country relied on these men. He also said that the policy, conceived after the revolution, of compensating those who had fought against the dictatorship had produced unwanted results: thousands of men, attracted by financial gain, had since bought rifles and taken charge of crossroads or national assets. The situation was now so grave, he said, that the numbers of those claiming to have fought on the winning side of the war had reached a quarter of a million.

When we first arrived, Marwan, the cousin who picked us up at the airport, jokingly told me that I could not have come at a better time, because he, as were most of Benghazi's judges, was on strike and therefore had all the time in the world to spend with me. He told me how, only the

49

week before, armed men had burst into the courtroom in the middle of a trial and, at gunpoint, forced the presiding judge to sign a release form for the accused. Many in the legal community – judges, lawyers and counsellors – feared reprisals. Marwan was busy investigating ways to pressure Tripoli to take the matter seriously. He took me to a couple of meetings, and I saw how he managed to rally the country's most respected judges into forming what eventually became the Libyan Judges' Organization, an NGO that monitors and campaigns for the independence of the judiciary.

Similar struggles were happening on various other fronts. I have never been anywhere where hope and apprehension were at such a pitch. Anything seemed possible, and nearly every individual I met spoke of his optimism and foreboding in the same breath.

*

When we entered Ajdabiya, we stopped at the main roundabout, renamed Tim Hetherington Square, after the British photojournalist who was killed covering the war in Misrata. We bought boxes of fruit. I felt that panic again at not knowing how to approach Libya. I stood beside the car as the fruit-seller loaded the boot. I recognized Ajdabiya's dry light, the blue of its empty sky, the way the heat holds you.

Uncle Mahmoud called my mobile. I told him we were only metres away, and when we reached the familiar street I saw him standing outside the house. He was tall and thin. My aunts clustered behind him. I embraced them first, and when they began to cry I knew they were crying for their missing brother. When Father's sisters want their husbands or their children to promise to do something, they ask them to swear not on God or His prophets but on my father, Jaballa. Uncle Mahmoud, with his mischievous smile, said, 'Come now, let's not turn it into a Turkish soap opera.' When I embraced him, I held on to his bony frame for a long while.

Not since my father's disappearance had I felt closer to him. My aunts have his eyes. All they wanted was to look at me, and all I wanted was to look at them. We sat next to one another and held hands. My father had beautiful hands like theirs, the skin cool and soft.

*

Light is no longer welcome in the houses. It is shut out, like other things that come from outdoors: dust, heat and bad news. Architecture, the physical representation of considered gestures, has changed here in the years I have been away. It has turned its back on nature. When I was a boy, gardens had low fences or no fences at all and, outside the high sun hours, windows would be left open. Now high brick walls keep out the view and windows are almost permanently shuttered. I could not help but read, in this new determination to keep out the sun and the passing gaze, an inner upheaval, a private disquiet. I often found myself in rooms where the shutters had not been opened for a long time. I was obliged at midday, and after several attempts at trying to convince the expanded wood to let go of its frame, to walk to the switch beside the door and turn on the lights. Lunch was often eaten under a chandelier. All this gave me the impression, when I opened the door and was faced with a wall of light and the blue above hovering like an upturned sea, that the line separating the interior and exterior here was like one of those transformative boundaries we read about in ancient myths.

After lunch, I sat with Uncle Mahmoud, the shutters closed against the sun. I thought about the endless questions I had for him. But he did not need me to encourage him; he wanted to speak about his time in prison. It was most of what we talked about. My uncle had spent twenty-one years in Abu Salim. And, like the things he had told me over the telephone when he was first released, his stories were aimed at proving that the authorities had failed, that he had not been erased, that he continued to remember and even managed to follow, through the radio the guards occasionally allowed him, what his nephew the novelist was up to in faraway London. His stories were an attempt to bridge the vast distance that separated the austere cruelty of Abu Salim and the world outside. Perhaps, like all stories, what Uncle Mahmoud's recollections were saying was: 'I exist.'

Uncle Mahmoud started by telling me about his first interrogation, a few minutes after his arrest. He had sat handcuffed in a room. He did not know its location. He was shown reams of paper: transcripts of every telephone call, no matter how insignificant, made from my family's home in Cairo. He was shown a large, six-drawer cabinet full of documents and photographs of my father in public places in Egypt, sometimes with my mother, my brother and me, at weddings, social gatherings, sitting in a restaurant, crossing a street. 'They knew everything,' Uncle Mahmoud said. They had been monitoring my father, with the help of the Egyptian authorities, for years. 'They did not tell me that they had Jaballa,' he said. 'It was the furthest thing from my mind.'

*

At 1 a.m., twelve hours after his arrest, Uncle Mahmoud was blindfolded and put in a truck. 'I still had no idea where we were,' he said. 'The truck began to move. The journey seemed to go on forever. Then we stopped. I was led off the truck. I was taken down to a basement. I thought perhaps they had brought me to those old Ottoman prison cells beneath Al-Saraya al-Hamra, in Tripoli. It turned out we were not underground at all, that we had only gone down a little ramp or something. They led me, turning left, right, left, right several times, until I was told to stop. 'Extend your hands.' I extended my hands. A man gave me a blanket. 'Extend your hands,' he said again, and handed me a mattress. Then he opened a door. This was the first time I heard the horrific noise – a noise that was to become familiar – of the heavy door, rusted or not opened in ten years, being unlocked and swung open. He pushed me in and slammed the door, bolting it shut. My hands were no longer handcuffed, but I still had the blindfold on. I feared what I might find, so I waited a few minutes before taking it off. I found myself in a place that was absolutely dark. Gradually, I began to see a little. I was terribly thirsty. It felt as if someone were telling me to turn around. I turned and found a tap. Clean, sweet water. I drank and thanked God. Slowly, like a cat's eyes, I began to see in the dark. I saw now that I was in a small room, four walls. I felt dizzy and still had no idea where I was exactly. I spread the mattress on the floor and, I'm not joking, I was asleep before my head touched it.

'I woke up in the morning to the sounds of two men speaking. I had no idea where I was, if this room was in a desert, standing alone, or part of a compound. One man called out, "Hamid," and the other said, "Yes, Saad." "Do you know where you are?" "No, where am I, Saad?" "You are in Abu Salim." That was how I learnt that I had fallen into this terrible place. We had all heard about Abu Salim. I had assumed the two men speaking were in the same room, perhaps beaten so badly that each had collapsed at either end of the cell. It turned out – and later I got used to the peculiar world of the prison – that they were in different cells, about five doors apart, in fact. I didn't have my glasses. I walked around the room to read up close the names and dates scratched into the walls. I then found a tiny hole in one of the walls. I looked through it and saw a man walking in a room very similar to mine. This was how I discovered I had a neighbour. He spotted me. He came close, looked through the hole and then said, "Uncle?" It was your cousin, Saleh.'

*

During those early few days, Uncle Mahmoud and Uncle Hmad and my cousins Saleh and Ali came to learn of each other's presence in the prison. Being in the same section, they could hear one another. 'Our wing was full,' Uncle Mahmoud told me. 'But the opposite wing was empty. Not a movement. Just one door that occasionally opened and shut. There was someone there. Who he was, no one knew. After seven days, we heard him. Every night, when the prison fell silent, he recited poetry late into the night. The poems belonged to a specific form, popular in Ajdabiya, often used in elegies because of its mournful repetition. The voice was that of an elderly man. We listened to him but didn't know who he was. One day, he called out my name. I answered, asking him who he was. "You don't recognize me?" he said. I told him, "No." He didn't speak after that. Do you know how long he fell silent for? A whole week. After that, he called my name again and asked if I still couldn't recognize him. "I will give you a clue," he said. "Your trousers are falling." This was a joke I'd had with your father from when we were children. I did not reply. I thought it must be a trap. I just couldn't imagine Jaballa being there. Another week passed before I heard him calling my name again. Ali called out and said, "It's Uncle Jaballa." Hmad said, "Don't believe him. Ask him for another sign." I did and he said, "I am from Blo'thaah." I felt sick, as if my heart had split.'

*

Just then we were interrupted. The door to the garden opened. Light entered as solid as a wall, blackening the three or four figures walking in. We stood up to greet them. Relatives and friends of the family. Tea was brought. Uncle Mahmoud went around the room serving it, I following behind with biscuits and nuts. The usual platitudes were repeated. Then the conversation settled on the security problems facing the country. The more passionate the exchanges, the quieter Uncle Mahmoud became. Now he responded to a question or a proclamation with a simple nod or a weary smile. He closed his eyes and fell asleep, his tea untouched.

6. Poems

The country that separates fathers and sons has disoriented many travellers. It is very easy to get lost here. Telemachus, Edgar, Hamlet and countless other sons, their private dramas ticking away in the silent hours, have sailed so far out into the uncertain distance between past and present that they seem adrift. They are men, like all men, who have come into the world through another man, a sponsor, opening the gate and, if they are lucky, doing so gently, perhaps with a reassuring smile and an encouraging nudge on the shoulder. And the fathers must have known, having once themselves been sons, that the ghostly presence of their hand will remain throughout the years, to the end of time, and that no matter what burdens are laid on that shoulder or the number of kisses a lover plants there, perhaps knowingly driven by the secret wish to erase the claim of another, the shoulder will remain forever faithful, remembering that good man's hand that had ushered them into the world. To be a man is to be part of this chain of gratitude and remembering, of blame and forgetting, of surrender and rebellion, until a son's gaze is made so wounded and keen that, on looking back, he sees nothing but shadows. With every passing day the father journeys further into his night, deeper into the fog, leaving behind remnants of himself and the monumental yet obvious fact, at once frustrating and merciful – for how else is the son to continue living if he must not also forget – that no matter how hard we try we can never entirely know our fathers.

I think this as I consider Uncle Mahmoud's account of learning that Father was not safely home in Cairo but a few metres away in a cell in the opposite wing. Like many of the stories I heard from men who were in prison at the same time, this one too offered more questions than it did answers. I wondered why Father waited so long before speaking. He had already been in Abu Salim for a few days, and must have heard uncles Mahmoud and Hmad, cousins Ali and Saleh, talking loudly across the cells. And why, once he had spoken and was not recognized, did he wait a whole week before trying again and then, after that second attempt failed, wait yet another seven days? What was he thinking about in that time? From where did the doubt or reticence stem? And why the secrecy; why not simply say 'Mahmoud, it's me, your brother, Jaballa'? On the other hand, I could not understand why Uncle Mahmoud and the others were unable to make out the voice of the man they knew so well. In fact, even before Father spoke directly to Uncle Mahmoud – calling out, 'Mahmoud, you don't recognize me?' – how could they not have realized that the man reciting poems at night was Jaballa Matar? They may not have recognized the voice, but how could they have missed the clue in the poems Father selected for those night-time recitations? Father's literary memory was like a floating library. It would have been unusual for him not to be able to recall at least one poem by every significant Arabic poet from the modern era. But in prison he did not go to the poems of Ahmed Shawqi or any of the numerous poets from the period of Al-Nahda, the so-called Arabic Renaissance that took place at the turn of the twentieth century, nor did he turn to Badr Shakir al-Sayyab or the various other modernist poets he admired. Instead, in those dark and silent nights when, as Uncle Mahmoud had put it, 'the prison fell so quiet you could hear a pin drop or a grown man weep softly to himself,' Father sought refuge in the elegiac Bedouin poetry of the alam. The word means 'knowledge' or 'banner' or 'flag', but has always, at least to my mind, signified an apprehension gained through loss. It's a poetic form that privileges the past over the present. It is popular across Cyrenaica, but no more so than in Ajdabiya.

I picture him reciting the alam in the same voice he used at home, a voice that seemed to open up a landscape as magically uncertain and borderless as still water welded to the sky. This happened rarely. It would often take several obliging individuals to get him to start. Friends would turn to him towards the end of one of those epic dinner parties my parents used to host at our Cairo flat. This stage in the evening, which always arrived too late, was for me the moment that made sense of all the preceding madness. It was like one of those villages perched high in the mountains, reached after too many dizzying turns and arguments: Mother saying, 'Enough, let's turn back,' and Father answering, 'But, look, we're nearly there.' Then the incline would flatten and we would be inside the village, protected from the vastness of the landscape.

First, there was the menu, which shifted several times before agreement was reached. And then the machinery would start. Every resource would be employed – servants, children and a handful of committed friends – until each desired ingredient was located and delivered. My mother managed this complicated operation with the authority of an artist in the service of a higher cause. She spent hours on the telephone, handing out precise instructions to the butcher, the farmer who brought us our milk, yoghurt and cheese, and the florist. She made several trips to the fruit-seller. She would drive into the Nile Delta, down narrow dirt roads, to a small village near Shibin El Kom in the Monufia Governorate, to select, as she used to say, 'with my own eye' each pigeon. I would be sent to get nutmeg from one spice shop west of the city, then gum arabic from another in the east. There was only one vegetable-seller in the whole of Cairo from whom to buy garlic at this time of the year. Several samples of pomegranate would be tasted before she placed the order. And because, she maintained, Egyptians have no appreciation for olive oil, she would order gallons from her brother's farm in the Green Mountain or, if the Libyan–Egyptian border was closed, from Tuscany or Liguria. Ziad and I would then have to accompany the driver to the airport to explain to the customs officials why our household consumed so much olive oil, pay the necessary bribes and return home to Mother's happy face. Orange blossom water was delivered from her hometown, Derna, or, if that wasn't possible, from Tunisia. On the day of the party, a dash of it would be put on to the pomegranate fruit salad and into the jugs of cold water. The marble tiles would be mopped with it too.

The combination of Mother's eccentricities and Father's wealth – he had made a small fortune importing Japanese and Western goods to the Middle East – meant not only that we could live lavishly but also that the money helped fuel Father's political activism. He set up a fund for Libyan students abroad and supported various scholarly projects, such as an Arabic translation of a legal encyclopaedia. But what made my father dangerous to the Qaddafi regime was that his financial resources matched his political commitment. He was a leader. He knew how to manage and organize a movement. He coordinated several sleeper cells inside Libya. He set up and led military training camps in Chad, close to the Libyan border. He did not only pour his own money into this; he also had a gift for raising large donations and would shuttle around the world convincing wealthy Libyan exiles to support his organization. Its annual budget in the early 1980s was $7 million. A few years later, by the late 1980s, that figure had gone up to $15 million. But he did not stop there. He personally commanded the small army in Chad.

Growing up, I had somehow always suspected that our money would all disappear. I worried about it. On more than one occasion I asked him, 'How much is left?'

'Well, Minister of Finance,' he would say, smiling. 'Let's just say it's none of your business.'

'But I want to make sure we'll be all right.'

'You'll be all right,' he would say. 'All I owe you is a university education. After that, you are on your own.'

After he was kidnapped, we found that the bank account was nearly empty. According to the statements, the balance in 1979, the year we left Libya, was $6 million. In little over a decade, it had all vanished. I felt terribly resentful, particularly since the day Father had disappeared, the countless so-called activists who used to float in and out of our flat, and even Father's closest allies, vanished. It was as though we had contracted a contagious disease. Most of all, I couldn't believe he would leave Mother, who had never worked a day in her life, without a proper income. Ziad and I had to immediately find ways to support the family. The only explanation I could think of was that Father must have been certain of imminent victory. He must have thought he and Mother would return to Tripoli, sell the Cairo flat and perhaps live off the land he had in Libya. It took me time to understand the implications of Father's actions. When it came to Mother, he considered Ziad and me as his guarantors. He believed he could rely on us. It was a profound gesture of trust. I know, not least of all from his letters, that from within his incarcerated existence, the thought of his sons brought him comfort and reassurance. He had given me something priceless: namely, his confidence. I am grateful I was forced to make my own way. His disappearance did put me in need and make my future uncertain, but it turns out need and uncertainty can be excellent teachers.

During the Cairo years when he was still here, we lived in a penthouse that occupied the entire top floor of a tall building in Mohandeseen. When we first moved in, you could see for miles, all the way to where Cairo ended and the farms took over. But very quickly high buildings rose all around us and left only narrow views on to the horizon. In preparation for those dinner parties, men would come and hang precariously off the ledge to wash the glazing that covered the whole wall at one end of the drawing room. On the day, the brass incense cup would be taken into every room, the smoke deposited in each corner, trapped behind curtains. The doorbell would not stop ringing with deliveries. The kitchen, which was off the main entrance, would have my mother at its centre, helped by the cook and a couple of maids. The radio would be on very loud, playing the songs of Farid al-Atrash or Najat al-Saghira or Oum Kalthum or Mohammad Abdel Wahab. My mother belonged to one of those Libyan families for whom Cairo was the cultural capital. She loved the city and moved in it with great ease. She would repeat what her mother used to say whenever she encountered a grim person: 'Don't blame them; they must've never been to Cairo.' In those days my mother operated as if the world were going to remain forever. And I suppose that is what we want from our mothers: to maintain the world – and, even if it is a lie, to proceed as though the world could be maintained. Whereas my father was obsessed with the past and the future, with returning to and remaking Libya, my mother was devoted to the present. For this reason, she was the truly radical force in my adolescence.

Ours was a political home, filled with dissidents and the predictable and often tiresome conversations of dissidents. These high dinners were my mother's retaliation against that reality. Her obsessiveness with where and when to get each ingredient, combined with her extraordinary talent as a cook, produced astonishing results that literally silenced these men of action. I would escape the activity and not return till evening. Mother would pull me into the kitchen, insisting I taste several of the dishes, asking if the salt was right, if she should not add more chilli. The table would be set so magnificently that guests would either be speechless or induced to such heights of pleasure that they could not stop talking. I remember once a gregarious man who had been a minister under King Idris. He had dominated the conversation until soup was served. He took the first mouthful and fell utterly silent. The entire table took note of the sudden change. 'All well, Minister?' Father asked. The man nodded without bringing his head up. He would occasionally dab his eyes with the napkin. I thought he was one of those men who break out in a sweat the moment they start eating. It wasn't until his plate was empty and he had no option but to look up that we saw his eyes were red. When the main course arrived, his emotion shifted to laughter. All this gave Mother great satisfaction, and, even though Father tried to hide it, his pride was clear. Those were the strong years, when my parents had the confident manner of couples that, notwithstanding the usual apprehensions of parents, regard the future as a friendly country.

And it was usually after one of those dinners that the welcome request would arise, spoken softly at first, then less timidly by another guest, before the insistent calls would grow into a loud clamour. Father's cheeks would redden slightly, his eyes betraying a twinkle of pleasure, and then he would yield. Nothing seemed to please him more than the presence of poetry. A good line reassured him, put the world right for a second. He was both enlivened and encouraged by language. It would become clear that his earlier resistance was merely to test the enthusiasm of his companions. He would lean slightly forward and it would happen: in that tentative silence, a new space would open up. He knew exactly what to do with his voice, where to tighten the strings and when to let them slacken. He always bracketed these recitations, perhaps out of reminiscence or loyalty to his hometown, with the alam.

He had, on several occasions, written in the genre. He recited them to me when he and I were alone in the car, which is to say, very rarely. My father hardly ever drove me to school, or to sports clubs, or collected me from a friend's house. Once, on my mother's insistence, he came to watch me compete in judo. I was distracted by how out of place he looked. He neither fitted in with, nor could altogether hide, his disinterest in Egyptian middle-class society. He almost never engaged in small talk or talking merely to pass the time. I cannot recall him speaking about money or property or the latest this or that. He had an astonishing ability to sustain social silences, which is why he was often mistaken for being haughty or cold. He was certainly proud. I recall him once saying to a member of the Egyptian government who was trying to convince him to quit politics: 'The only thing standing between you and me is a suitcase. If I'm no longer welcome here, I'll pack tomorrow.' He taught my brother and me to never accept financial assistance from anyone, especially governments, and when giving to give so discreetly that your 'left hand does not know what the right hand has done'. Once he saw me count change before handing it to a beggar. 'Next time, don't make a display of it,' he said. 'Give as if you were taking.' It took me a long time to understand this. If we passed labourers or street-sweepers eating their lunch and they invited us to join them, which was the custom – meaning they never expected you to actually join them – Father would sit in his fine clothes on the ground amongst the men and, if I was not as quick as he was, he would say, 'Come, an honest meal feeds a hundred.' He would take a bite or two, then conduct his magic trick, sliding bank notes beneath the plate mid-sentence. He would look at the time and say, 'Men, you are excellent, thank you.' His voice, which was always gentle, would rise if he learnt that one of the servants had turned away a needy person or shooed off a cat. The simple rule was never to refuse any one or thing in need. 'It's not your job to read their hearts,' he once told me after I claimed, with shameful certainty, that begging was a profession. 'Your duty is not to doubt but to give. And don't ask questions at the door. Allow them only to tell you what they came for after they've had tea and something to eat.' The word got around. Our doorbell would ring two or three times a day. Most people needed money for food or school or medicine. Some wanted us to mediate in a dispute, to return to them a piece of property – a wagon, a bicycle, a basket – that someone had confiscated after an argument. My brother and I would often manage this without my father's involvement, as if it were part of our education. It thinned the walls of our privilege a little and taught me something of the injustice and humiliation of being in need. The other thing he insisted on was that we learn how to ride a horse, shoot a rifle and swim. It was something his father, Grandfather Hamed, believed and, I suspect, took from Umar ibn al-Khattab. Father would drive me into the desert on the edge of Cairo, beyond the Giza Pyramids, to teach me how to handle a rifle. It was on such rare afternoons, when we were alone in the car, that he would recite to me his new compositions. If I teased him, he would say, 'They are masterpieces; you would've known this had you not been an ignorant boy,' which made me laugh like nothing else.

Uncle Mahmoud knew all of these details. In fact, given Father's intention to covertly inform him of his presence, it is very probable that Father had chosen one of his own poems to recite, perhaps the one that starts:

> Had the pain not been so precise
> I would have asked
> To which of my sorrows should I yield.

Uncle Mahmoud blamed his failure to recognize his brother's voice on the general confusion of prison life, the shock of his capture, the endless interrogations, the disorienting confinement. 'Such circumstances,' he said, 'tamper with your cognitive powers.'

He could detect that I was not entirely convinced.

'In the end,' he added, 'I just didn't want to believe it.'

But shock and the refusal to accept bad news can only partly explain it. I was gradually surrendering to the only explanation that seemed credible. Father wanted to be recognized just by his voice. To be known without needing to provide any more evidence. Perhaps, like me, what was uppermost in his mind was preservation. Part of what we fear in suffering – perhaps the part we fear most – is transformation. I still have recurring dreams in which I appear to him as a stranger. One of these took place only months after his disappearance and yet I have never forgotten it. In it, Father had undergone an experience so extreme that he could not recognize me. He looked at me as if we did not know each other. Therefore, perhaps Uncle Mahmoud's inability to recognize Father was not only due to the bewildering effects of prison life but also to Father having become a changed man. And perhaps Uncle Mahmoud knew this but did not want to say it out loud. Perhaps on hearing his brother's voice, Uncle Mahmoud's response was like that of Dante when, descending into the depths of hell, the poet comes upon Ciacco, a man he had known in the life before but who was now completely unrecognizable, and tells him:

> ... 'The anguish you endure
> Perhaps effaces whatever memory I had,

> Making it seem I have not seen you before;
>   But tell me who you are, assigned to so sad
>   A station as punishment – if any is more
> Agony, none is so repellent.'

Like Dante, Uncle Mahmoud must have known it was my father's voice, and, like Ciacco, Father was hoping to prove to himself that he was who he had been.

7. Your health? Your family?

The question of what Father went through during his captivity continues to haunt me. My mind fixes on the early days, the first few hours. It is as if my imagination, when focused on his life in prison, enters a fog. I am only able to see into a shallow distance. In the first couple of years, the thought alone of what Father was going through restricted me. We were repeatedly warned by the Egyptian authorities – who, to keep us silent, led us to believe that they had him at a secret location on the outskirts of Cairo – that if we campaigned or, in their words, 'made too much noise', it would 'complicate the situation'. We believed them. I was nineteen. I turned into a bridled animal, cautious and quiet. I could not stop thinking of the detestable things that were surely happening to my father as I bathed, as I sat down to eat. I stopped speaking. I hardly left my London flat except to go to my lectures at the university or to the National Gallery. I flew back to Cairo, and, because this was a delayed reaction, more than a year after the event, I had no words to explain it. I remained indoors for six months. Eventually, passing from one room to the other became a complicated activity. The threshold would begin twisting. I can still see the frame of the arch between the living room and the hall bending maniacally the closer I approached. Any repeti-

tive movement increased my heartbeat. Looking out of
the window, I had to make sure my eyes did not land on
the wheels of a passing car. The sight of that revolution
for a fraction of a second would leave me trembling. One
day, provoked by something my mother or brother had
said – the cause remains obscure in my memory – my leg
began to repeatedly kick the underside of the table in the
kitchen. The heavy wooden thing kept pulsing up and
down, the plates on it jumping and landing nearly, but not
quite, where they had been before. Ziad held me and
unjustly admonished Mother, 'See what you have done?'
He felt responsible for her and me, and I felt responsible
for him and her, and she for us all. Each one was parent
and child. To make up for the missing pillar, the once balanced structure of four columns was now in perpetual
strain.

*

When Uncle Mahmoud opened his eyes, the guests did
not notice but continued to chat in loud voices. He smiled
at me through their exchanges. More visitors arrived. Second and third cousins. I did not know them, and they did
not know me, but we embraced and sat, talking, exchanging polite enquiries about one another's lives. I felt
recognized. I was convinced that if I packed all my belongings and appeared at their door they would take me in.
This was an odd thought, particularly given how nervous
a house-guest I am and how I usually try to avoid staying
with other people. This is the drunkenness of return, I

told myself. The symptoms will wear off soon. More tea, coffee and sweets were served. Some smoked in silence, and others looked down at their laps or studied their fingers. When the excitement and nerves left us with nothing to say, we did what most people do and Libyan Bedouin society excels at: we repeated platitudes that were courteous and impersonal, questions that, the etiquette here dictates, ought never to be specific. The main purpose is to steer clear of what the male members of my paternal family are always careful to avoid: intrusion and gossip. They distrust people who speak too much. As a result you can end up in situations where the conversation consists of a few sentences that are repeated ad infinitum, as happened with an elderly man who came after all the other visitors had left. He was slight, dressed in an old black English wool coat buttoned up to the collar. He had on a white turban that, although turned loosely around the shape of his head, seemed in no danger of slipping off. Either from the assumption that I knew who he was or else from the desire to ignore the 33-year handicap that divided me from them, no one introduced us. In some indefinable way, he was familiar. He held me by the arms and then without saying a word proceeded to look at me. His eyes were green and opaque like jade. His face, like his body, indulged no excess: thin, handsome, with a short, pure white moustache and beard. His skin was dark, leathery red, and the lines in it many and a slightly paler colour. We embraced. I let go before he did. I hugged him again and this time made sure that my strength matched his. He pulled me to sit beside him. He wrapped my arm around his and, smiling, continued to look into my eyes. He asked me nothing about my life. All he said was, 'Are you well? Your health? Your family?' and would repeat these three questions every two minutes or so.

'Haj, you disappeared,' Uncle Mahmoud said, I suspected more to break the monotony.

The man continued facing me, but his smile showed mischief now.

His son, an urbane-looking man about my age, began teasing his father. 'His condition has grown severe,' he said to Uncle Mahmoud. 'Now the maximum he can bear us for is a day, maybe two.'

'Where do you go?' I asked him, but, because of our close physical proximity and the fact that we were sitting to one side of the gathering, I spoke softly, which made it seem as if he and I were conspiring against the others.

He smiled and nodded, as though to say, 'Pay no mind to their silliness.' The gesture seemed also to mean 'It will all pass.'

'He goes into the desert,' his son said, slightly blushing as he spoke and looking at me, in that way relatives I hardly know but who are close in age often do, with a shyness that both fears and desires my judgement. 'He goes to be with his camels. He loves them more than his own family. Spoils them rotten.'

The man continued looking at me, refusing to comment.

Uncle Mahmoud tried to speak for him: 'Who can blame him? He's tired of people.'

We continued sitting in the silence that followed, my

arm wrapped around his, his big hand gripping mine. He continued staring at me. I looked at him or at the others or at the floor or at his large hand on top of mine. His skin was like wood, his nails black. In contrast, my hand looked new and unused. 'Are you well? Your health? Your family?' he asked again. I attempted, this time, to answer thoroughly, but he was not interested in the information I was providing. His questions continued and seemed more ridiculous yet also more poignant with each repetition. Together with his silence, his eyes – those eyes not leaving mine, not looking anywhere else but into my own – made me feel I had entered, and was somehow trapped inside, a state as pure as an allegory. He wanted nothing from my existence except itself.

When he and his son left, Uncle Mahmoud told me who he was:

'Muftah, your father's cousin. They were very close. He prefers to be at Blo'thaah with the camels. As kids he and your father used to play there. He was with your father when your uncle Salah died.'

'Who is Uncle Salah?'

'Our older brother. He was one year older than your father, and one day he stepped on a mine that the Italians or the Germans or the English had left there. Your father was ten. He was spared only because he had gone off to pee. But the sight of Salah blown up traumatized him for a long time.'

Returning home after decades, I was confronted with such stories told with the casualness of an old anecdote and, as with this one, the information is shocking exactly because it was somehow anticipated. There was always a sense about my father, quietened and trained by the years of sustained grief, together with a certain distance from his relations, particularly from some of his siblings, that I could now see might have arisen from the gap left by that fallen brother.

'The desert there is still scattered with mines. Muftah was there too and saw what happened. He loved your father. You can tell, no?'

8. The Truce and the Clementine

The guests left. Uncle Mahmoud and I were alone again. His energy picked up. He was playful with his children, laughed loudly at their jokes. He was quicker than his sons, the first to carry plates back to the kitchen after a meal, the first to detect who was yet to have fruit, bouncing up to hand them the bowl. Only in the background, in some secret compartment of his being, did there seem to be a quiet, resolute withdrawal, a shyness not too unlike that of a believer who, once having had his faith challenged, was now resigned to nursing his convictions in secret. At times, in mid-conversation, his thoughts brought him to a sudden silence. When the call to prayer was heard, he would take himself to the corner of the room and, without the practice now fashionable across the Arab world of worshippers encouraging others to join them, spread a mat and softly conduct his prayers. His posture then – his pencil frame, the boyish agility of his movements – seemed to be an effort against erasure. It was at once specific yet part of our old human struggle against mortality. It cast a distance between him and the world that, like the fan shape the fisherman's net leaves when it touches the surface of the water, was only momentarily perceptible.

Perhaps Uncle Mahmoud had called a truce – the specific

terms of which were known only to him, or maybe not even known consciously – one of those silent manoeuvres intended to veil us from a world of infinite danger. I wondered at what point it had taken place. Perhaps it was during the disappointed activity of mealtime, or in an empty moment captured inside a casual hour – if indeed casual hours exist in prison – walking in the courtyard under the enormous sun in the years when he was allowed out of the cell, pacing the long rectangular dirt ground, remembering to himself, or recounting to a fellow-inmate, in the animated style for which Uncle Mahmoud remains well known, certain details of *The Brothers Karamazov* or *Candide* or *Madame Bovary* or any of the novels he loves, and doing so out of the same desire that leads free men to reread books: to replicate and deepen the pleasure. Or perhaps it was not a novel but a football match – for, although, like his older brother, Uncle Mahmoud's enthusiasms for football and literature are distinct in quality, they are equal in intensity. I picture him now walking under the sun, recounting to a friend, out of the wish to awaken the happy memory, the details of the last football match he had watched with my father, which took place on the 13th of September 1989, exactly six months before the two brothers were imprisoned. I was attending university in London and therefore could not be in Cairo for Uncle Mahmoud's momentous visit, the first since we had left Libya a decade before. The Libyan regime had forbidden nearly all of my father's family from travelling outside the country. It was one of several tactics the authorities employed to punish my father and, by extension, his family. On account of Father's politics, it was almost impossible for any male member of my paternal family (except for the odd exception who was loyal to the regime) to gain employment or receive a scholarship. Given the large number of uncles and cousins I have, many were affected by this. And, not wishing to strengthen the association and cause them more problems, we did not call or write to members of our paternal family. In fact, I had not heard Uncle Mahmoud's voice since we had left Libya.

The afternoon he arrived in Cairo the telephone in my London flat rang. His voice was still familiar. It was as if, for the past ten years, it had been stored in my head. It seemed a little deeper and more rooted somehow. Although, of course, not having spoken to my uncle since I was eight, it was my vocal cords that, out of the two of us, had undergone the more dramatic transformation. He kept repeating, 'Oh, my God, Hisham, you sound like a grown man.' I spoke to Aunt Zaynab, the woman he married after we left the country. I wondered what she was like, what my parents made of her. The couple brought with them the newest member of the family, their baby son, Izz al-Arab Matar. Instead of the usual weekly long-distance call, I now telephoned Cairo nearly every day.

Uncle Mahmoud's visit that autumn coincided with the European Cup. Only reading took charge of Father's passions more intensely than football. And no team gave him more pleasure than Bayern Munich. When Father was away on work, my mother videotaped every one of their matches. She continued doing so after he was kidnapped, recording not only those of the German team but every football match broadcast, no matter how inconsequential, including Egypt's Second Division tournament. Every time I came home on holidays, I would find the library of videotapes had grown by a metre. Each was labelled with not the usually careful turns of Mother's handwriting, but a hurried version of it, noting quickly the competing teams – 'Mali–Senegal', 'Cameroon–Egypt', 'Juventus–Barcelona' – and the date. She only stopped when we received the first of Father's prison letters, three years later. By then she had recorded hundreds of hours of football, which, I remember calculating, if Father had returned to us then with his passion for football intact, it would have taken several years for him to watch.

But those were still happy days. My parents were reunited with Father's dearest sibling, who, on account of the sixteen years that separated them, was brother and son to my father, and were meeting their sister-in-law and the new-born nephew who, to Father, must have been the closest he had ever come to holding a grandson.

In the first round of the European Cup that year, Bayern Munich met Glasgow Rangers. Minutes before kick-off, my mother was, in her usual way, trying to decide which side to support. Like me, she had settled on Rangers not only to give Father and Uncle Mahmoud the pleasure of adversaries but also because Rangers had the only black player on the field.

'His name is Mark Walters,' I told Mother over the telephone. 'He's only two years older than Ziad,' I said.

'Is he African?' Mother asked.

'I don't know but he's the first black player to ever play for Rangers. His first match was a scandal. Supporters shouted and spat at him. Thousands of bananas were thrown on the pitch.'

I exaggerated. Bananas were indeed thrown during Mark Walters's first match, but not thousands.

Mother handed me to Uncle Mahmoud. I gave him the same information about Mark Walters. He paused, then said what he would often say when we spoke on the telephone: 'It's a real shame you're not here.' Then, 'Your cousin Izzo says hello,' even though we both knew that Izzo, at only ten months old, was incapable of saying much at all. He handed me to Father.

'Where will you watch it?' he asked.

'At a friend's place,' I lied.

I hung up and went to the local pub, ordered a pint and sat with strangers watching the match. Twenty-five minutes into the game, Rangers were awarded a penalty. Mark Walters was to take it. I watched him walking back from the ball. I began reciting Surat al-Fatiha. Here was an eighteen-year-old Arab Muslim praying in an English pub for a Scottish team because they had a black player who might or might not have been African, while his Libyan family, exiled in Cairo, were rooting for a German team. Thank God, Mark Walters scored. Two minutes later Bayern Munich equalized. Final score was 3–1 in favour of the Germans. It did not matter; it was not the black man's fault.

After the match I called home again. Father, who was rarely the one to answer, picked up.

'I knew it was you,' he said. 'Did you see the artistry? Pure genius. Here; your uncle wants you.'

'Hisham, listen, your cousin is a born Bayern supporter. He started crying the moment your African friend … What's his name?' I could hear Mother in the background, saying, 'Mark Walters', spoken as if the name belonged to a great philosopher or poet. 'Izzo screamed the moment this Mark Walters scored.'

*

Recently, Izzo's younger sister, Amal, born the year after Uncle Mahmoud and Aunt Zaynab's visit, located a photograph with the date, in orange digits in the bottom-right-hand corner, 13/09/89: the same day as the Bayern–Rangers match. It shows ten-month-old Izzo on my father's knee. The child's miniature hand is reaching towards a clementine that Father is tempting him with. Father is wearing his dark blue farmala, the traditional Libyan suit. I recall choosing the wool with him, and taking it to the tailor in Cairo's old district of Khan el-Khalili. Father's hand – it is difficult to convey the effect that seeing Father's hand can still have on me – occupies the centre of the photograph, holding between the tips of his fingers the bright clementine. Izzo's eyes are on the fruit; Father's are on the camera and therefore on us or, I should say, on me. In the foreground is the fruit bowl; to the right of Father are the legs of another man. From their slender and long frame, I suspect they belong to Uncle Mahmoud. He is wearing an identical farmala. Father must have taken him to his tailor. I wonder if the two brothers had stopped for lunch at the restaurant I took Father to when I accompanied him to the tailor. It was in one of the back alleys, up a narrow flight of stone steps. I remember Father following me up, saying, 'But where are you taking us?' and feeling that thrill as I introduced my old man to something new and unusual, enjoying the quizzical expression on his face as he navigated the old broken steps, his fine leather shoes scraping the stone, and that readiness of his, wanting to prove that, no matter his fine tastes, he was still a man of the people. It always pleased him to know that I had my own way. When we entered the old working-class eatery, he greeted everyone, wishing them good appetite. They watched us with an expression of curiosity and amusement. And we were of course foreign, in nationality and class. The difference was clearer for him than for me, because by then I had perfected the Egyptian dialect and could pass for a Cairene, which, given the locals' exceptional talent in detecting a foreigner, was a feat that attracted the admiration of several family friends and the displeasure of our Libyan relatives. 'You order,' he said when we sat down. I got us the special: grilled goat chops. It reminded him of the Libyan dish mardoma, where the meat is slowly cooked in cinders. We ate well. 'I'll never find this place again,' he said as we were leaving. I stood him in the middle of the alleyway and pointed out the silver shop on the corner, the large brass lantern blackened with age on the opposite side, the old man selling pickled lupins and the sign above him that read MERCI-FUL. Father took note of all of these markers, but then repeated, 'I'll never find it.' But perhaps taking Uncle Mahmoud to the tailor had reminded him of our meal together and the location of the restaurant. Very few restaurants there serve goat meat. If he had asked, he would have been led to it.

*

Six months after the photograph was taken, Father and Uncle Mahmoud were arrested and Izzo was separated from his father. They met briefly in 2001, when the authorities decided to put Uncle Mahmoud and the others on trial. Hearing of the news, the families of the accused rushed to the courthouse and, for the first time in more than eleven years, laid eyes on their men. Izzo was thirteen. Uncle Mahmoud remembers the day vividly: 'I was standing with Hmad, Ali, Saleh and all the others in the dock, surrounded by high bars. The judge read out our names, including your father's name. Jaballa was described as the commander of our group. His whereabouts, the judge said, were "unknown".'

Shortly after the trial, one of my cousins sent me a copy of the transcript of the court's proceedings. I remember reading the word 'unknown', and thinking, I know what that means: it means they killed him. But then hope, cunning and persistent, crept back in, and I convinced myself that because the Egyptian government had handed over my father on the condition that, as Father puts it in his first letter from prison, 'I never see the light', the court was doing what the authorities had done: they were hiding the fact that Jaballa Matar was in their custody. But now, hearing Uncle Mahmoud use that word, I was jolted once more, annoyed at my inability to resist hope. One needs to be vigilant with such a fate, I thought, looking out for the smallest clue, words that arise after long silences, words such as 'unknown'. Thinking this, I became convinced that Uncle Mahmoud too knew what this word meant. Instead of leaving it there, I could not help asking the stupid question:

'But this means they killed him?'

'I don't know,' Uncle Mahmoud said. 'I don't believe so. I still believe Jaballa is alive.'

'But how could that be?' I said, feeling myself grow impatient. 'If he is alive, then where is he?'

'I don't know,' he said. 'All I know is that he's my brother and I don't believe he's dead.' Then he told me what he had told me over the telephone the day he was released: 'Don't lose hope.' And with that he returned to telling me about the day in the courtroom, the day he saw his son, Izzo, for the first time in eleven years.

'We were all charged with treason,' he said. 'We weren't assigned a defence and there was confusion in the court-room as to who was going to address the charge. At that moment women and children began coming into the room, peering towards us. I immediately spotted Zaynab. I did my best to look strong. I couldn't recognize the children. They had all grown so . . .'

'And Izzo?' I asked.

'He approached the dock with Zaynab and the children.

He was tall, thirteen years old, and very shy. I tried to joke with him.'

A couple of days after this conversation with Uncle Mahmoud, Uncle Hmad Khanfore described that scene to me. Unlike Uncle Mahmoud, he could not see his family in the crowd.

'I watched the people,' he said, 'and I was asking myself, how after so long will the children know their fathers? The man beside me had been in prison for exactly the same length of time as the rest of us. He had a strange affliction that meant he stopped breathing whenever he experienced a strong emotion. Anything that made him laugh or cry could stop him breathing. Whenever this happened, the only way to help him was to slap him hard on the back. The courtroom was very loud by this stage, with people calling out to their relatives, so I spoke into his ear. I told him, "See that fellow over there, that teenager looking at us? Well, he would have been a boy when his father was arrested. I bet you, if he is here looking for his father, that he wouldn't recognize him – how could he?" "Nonsense," the man said. "How could anyone not recognize his own father?" I waved to the teenager to come. "Who are you here to see?" I asked him. The boy said he had come to see his father. "Very well," I said. "And who is your father, what is his name?" The teenager answered, "His name is Hmad Khanfore." The man beside me fainted,' Uncle Hmad said, laughing. 'He collapsed to the ground and no beating on the back could help. The comedy continued, because my nervousness made me silly. So there I was telling tired old jokes to the son who could not recognize me.' Uncle Hmad laughed and I laughed with him. Then he stopped and said, 'We don't even know our children.'

The accused were convicted of conspiring against the state. My father was sentenced to death in absentia. The rest all got life. They were, from time to time, allowed visits after that. That was how, over the years, Izzo got to know his father a little.

9. The Old Man and His Son

Amal has become obsessed with Izzo. Nearly every day she posts at least one photograph of her brother on Facebook, pictures made available for anyone to see. Izzo as a young boy, with eyes curious and shy; Izzo by the sea, the blue pulsing behind him, not minding the wind in his hair, looking at us through a teenager's face newly conscious of adulthood yet not quite resigned to it. Then there are those of Izzo the freedom fighter. These form the majority of the pictures Amal has been posting: tens of photographs taken in the six months he fought in the armed rebellion against the dictatorship. They show him carrying a Kalashnikov, an RPG, his chest crossed with bullet belts. They show him driving a pick-up truck that has lost its doors. Knowing he is being watched, he looks as shy and pensive as a young man off on a trip with people he hardly knows. Then he is resting on a thin, browned mattress in some bombed-out building, probably in the latter months of the fighting, because beneath the well-worn yellow T-shirt his torso looks more muscular. In another he is standing against a broken-down wall. The house had been destroyed, but this part of the wall, like a map of an unknown country, stands, persisting. It keeps his shadow. Then there is a series of him showing his wounds: a face freckled by shrapnel, white cotton in the ears, pupils as red as plums. Over the six months of the war, his expression changes a little. In the early days he has the earnest sense of purpose of those who are anxious to do well. That keen desire to succeed remains but is gradually erased by a new fatigue that enters the eyes and fastens the eyebrows. A veil of bewilderment has fallen, endured and enduring. Something has changed, and, although perhaps it won't last forever, it seems limitless. Looking at these pictures, I hear his voice repeat, 'Is it too late? Perhaps it is too late,' and I know that what he means has nothing to do with retreating but is a response to the nature of war, the momentum sustained by conflict.

*

A few months before these war pictures were taken, Izzo was in his final year at university, studying to become a civil engineer. When my long years of campaigning for the release of my relatives coincided with the dictatorship's last-minute attempts to avoid a popular uprising, Uncle Mahmoud was one of several political prisoners released in early February 2011. For the first time since Izzo was a toddler, he was sleeping and waking up in the same house as his father. The news of Uncle Mahmoud's release had caused a huge traffic jam in Ajdabiya. Hundreds of well-wishers descended on the family. They came from neighbouring villages and towns and some from as far away as the capital, Tripoli. To many it offered a safe opportunity for an act of protest. No one could have known then that a fortnight later several towns and cities were going to rise in open revolt against the dictatorship.

Ajdabiya was amongst the first. The city changed hands three times. But on every occasion, what Qaddafi's tanks could not secure was the narrow network of streets at the heart of the city. When the fighting was at its fiercest, the women, children and elderly were moved to the relative safety of Benghazi. Uncle Mahmoud refused to leave. As all lines of communication were down, I sent him, through a journalist friend who was going to report on the war, a satellite telephone. When eventually we spoke, he said, 'The time for retreat has passed. We either win or I'll meet my end here. No one dies before his time. Besides, your uncle is not as old as you think. I can fight, and I'm a good cook. Here I can be useful to the boys.' I knew he didn't want to leave Izzo, who was taking part in the street battles around the family house. For Izzo, the war started on his doorstep.

When the city was secure, Izzo, along with several other young men from Ajdabiya, travelled the eighty kilometres east to Brega, a town that sits at the southernmost point of the Mediterranean Sea. Once Brega was won, the next destination was Misrata, Libya's third-largest city, some 600 kilometres west of Brega. Misrata was witnessing some of the bloodiest battles. It was widely believed then that if Misrata fell, Qaddafi would win the war, and if the rebels kept the city, they would have a strong base from which to organize the march westwards to the capital, Tripoli. Misrata therefore became existentially important to both sides of the conflict. Between Brega and Misrata was Qaddafi's stronghold city of Sirte, making it too dangerous for Izzo to travel by land. Along with other fighters, ammunition and what medical supplies they could gather, Izzo boarded a small, crowded fishing boat and, like the recent migrants who regularly abandon the continent at Libyan ports such as Brega, he made the slow, precarious progress north. On account of the blond-white desert that loops up on either side of Brega, the waters there are some of the most luminous in the Mediterranean Sea. But the further the boat went, the darker and thicker the sea would have become. Once they gained a safe distance from the Gulf of Sirte, they turned west. The landing at Misrata must have been exhilarating. I can picture Izzo, with his usual affability, embracing brothers-in-arms. Perhaps they seemed familiar to him. Perhaps he recognized himself in them. Or perhaps he saw in their faces what I now, looking at the photographs, see in his.

*

The fighting in Misrata dragged on. Qaddafi's desperation to recapture the city was matched by the determination of the resistance. We all came to know the names of the streets, the ingenious resourcefulness of the men and women of the city. Trucks that a few days before had been used to carry goods from the port were now driven down to the sea and filled with sand. What up to then had been regarded as a plentiful and useless material, carpeting the beaches and the surrounding desert landscape, begrudged for not being verdant, suddenly became an asset. The trucks were then driven into Tripoli Street and Benghazi Street, the two main avenues leading to the centre, and parked sideways. The wheels were punctured and the engines disabled. Qaddafi's tanks could not enter Misrata. That those two streets were named after Libya's other two major cities gave the revolutionaries the strength to fight for the whole country. Suddenly the names of our streets mattered. The inhabitants of Misrata knew their city well, which seemed to confirm that the people and not the dictatorship were the true custodians of Libya.

Whenever there was a lull in the fighting, Izzo would make the sea journey back to Brega, then the hour-drive to Ajdabiya, to rest, eat his mother's food and collect a clean set of clothes. There are photographs of him standing in the kitchen in military fatigues, holding a machine-gun, his face tired. He looked trapped, as if he had entered a tunnel and knew that the time for turning back had passed. On his last visit he tried to make his mother laugh, parodying the dictator's speech given a few days after the rebellion began, in which Qaddafi called on his supporters to march until 'the country is cleansed of the rats.'

'Mama,' Izzo said. 'Forward, forward.'

'But forward till when?' Aunt Zaynab asked him.

'Till Bab al-Azizia,' he told her.

Bab al-Azizia was the military compound in Tripoli where Qaddafi lived. We had heard stories, which always seemed too fanciful to be believed, that beneath the compound lay underground prisons where the dictator's most ardent dissidents were kept. Those accounts turned out to be true. Qaddafi liked to keep his strongest opponents nearby in order to be able to take a look at them from time to time: both the living and the dead. Freezers were discovered there with the bodies of long-deceased dissidents. 'I have a feeling,' Izzo told Aunt Zaynab, 'that Uncle Jaballa is there.' Izzo believed he would find my father alive.

*

On these brief visits home, Izzo showed his parents photos he took on his mobile phone of friends at the front. In most of these he looks earnest and out of place. He seems at ease only when he is with Marwan al-Towmi. The two met in Misrata and quickly became inseparable. One of their fellow-fighters told me later, 'When you found one, you knew the other was nearby. They always went into battle side by side. They trusted each other and knew they could rely on that.' Marwan was an economics graduate from Benghazi, and seven years Izzo's senior. In photographs his exceptionally tall, slim figure is always leaning slightly to one side, like a windswept pine. When photographed by Izzo, he is smiling playfully with the expression of one who has just shared a joke, or facing the camera with a look of quiet assurance.

There is a sequence of pictures showing them both in what appears to be a hallway connecting several rooms. The building is old and dilapidated. The walls, having once been blue, are an azure that glows oddly, as though it were frescoed. The ground is bare earth. There is a white plastic chair in the corner, not the flimsy sort commonly found today in Libya but one of those solid modernist Italian garden chairs you used to get in the 1970s. Two new-looking mattresses wrapped in an art deco black-and-white pattern are spread on the floor. They are so thin that they could not have made much of an improvement on the hard ground. Izzo is asleep on one, his head resting on an old lumpy pillow; its gauzy casing shows the dark forms of the stuffing. On the other mattress, Marwan is sitting up. His hands are just out of view; perhaps he is reading a book or cleaning a gun. In another picture, clearly taken only moments later, because the direction of the light coming in from the window has not changed that much, the arrangement is reversed: Marwan is now the one fast asleep, and Izzo is lying in the same place but awake, staring up at the ceiling. Both men are darker, sunburnt from the fighting. Even though there must have been at least one other person there, the man who took the photographs, they seemed to trust only each other to keep watch.

*

By the summer of that year, 2011, the fighting in Misrata had reached such a state of equilibrium that it seemed the war could go on forever. Sixty kilometres to the west, Zliten became of immense strategic importance to both sides. To Qaddafi loyalists, the coastal town was a crucial channel for reinforcements heading for Misrata and a major barrier guarding Tripoli. Zliten could help them turn the tide of rebellion. To the revolutionaries, winning Zliten would secure Misrata and offer a base from which to continue the march westward on to the capital. Whoever had Zliten was likely to win the war.

Back in February 2011, at the outset of the revolution, spontaneous popular protests had erupted in Zliten. They were quickly and ruthlessly quashed. Several months later, in early May, another peaceful protest was violently suppressed. The protestors made contact with rebels in Misrata, who supplied them with arms. On the 9th of June there was an armed assault on the military garrison in Zliten. I remember the day well because, in my efforts to supply international journalists with information about what was happening in Libya, I got the telephone number of a man involved in the attack. All I knew was that up to then he had been a diplomat and that his name (I was only given his first name) was Hisham.

When I called he said, 'I was expecting you. How are you? It is a real pleasure. And your family? Are they all well?'

He said this in the same automatic way in which such platitudes are often delivered, but in this context, hearing them spoken through a current of fear, by a man who sounded about my age and with whom I shared a name, unnerved me. My emotions were so sudden and intense that all I could do was plunge straight into the usual questions I had come to ask during those days: questions about when and how and what, the exact time, the numbers of those involved, the casualties, how many dead. During those days my flat in London had become a makeshift newsroom, where, together with a couple of friends, we were making up to fifty calls a day to men like Hisham, who were either part of the fighting or were bearing witness to it. Hisham was taken aback by my brisk manner, but he answered my questions in the same courteous tone he had used at the beginning of the conversation.

'We pushed them back. It's quiet now.' Then after a pause he said, 'They'll be back. They ran too quickly,' and repeated, 'They'll be back.' He sounded breathless, I assumed from fear, but then he said, 'I have to go. The troops can come back at any moment. Before they do, we must bury the dead.'

'How many?' I asked.

'Twenty-two.'

'Where are you burying them?'

'Here,' he said. He sounded like a man who had just realized he was trapped. 'In the square.'

*

I called Hisham several times every day after that but didn't manage to get hold of him till about one week later. I was relieved he was OK. This time I asked about his family. He said, 'Everyone is fine,' then shot the same questions back at me. We were suddenly speaking as if there were no war. 'Are you having a good day?' he asked.

I remember once hearing a conductor say that he had always, ever since he was a young boy, heard music in his head and that it wasn't until he was an adult that he realized this was not the same for everyone else. That has been my experience too, but with words and images. And in my conversation with Hisham I saw sunlight on a wall, a woman's hand, shadows of trees on the ground, a shut window with the sun lighting up the particles that clung to the pane, and I heard the sound of cloth being beaten outdoors, as though someone were airing linen, and the words 'together' and 'maybe' and 'I am'.

'They dug up the graves and burnt the bodies,' he said. He began to tell me of an elderly man in the town but then stopped. 'Do you want to speak to him?' he asked.

'Who dug up the bodies?'

'Qaddafi's men, of course,' he said in a mildly offended tone. 'Reinforcements arrived in buses. The situation here is very bad.'

I didn't know what to say.

'Do you want to speak to the old man? I have his number here,' he said, and without waiting for an answer he began reading it out. 'Wait two minutes, then call. Tell him you are my friend.'

Without knowing anything about the old man or why Hisham wanted me to call him, I looked at my watch until exactly two minutes had passed, then dialled the number. An old voice answered straight away.

'Welcome, my son,' he said. He sounded like he was unaccustomed to speaking on the telephone.

'Hisham asked me to call,' I said. 'We are friends.'

'But what can you do? No one can do anything.'

'What happened?' I asked.

'I watched them from my window. They came with bulldozers and dug up the graves, one after the other.

They burnt the corpses, and now everyone is afraid to touch them.' Then he said, 'But, thanks be to God, my son is here.'

'He's safe?' I asked.

'Yes. He's in his room. The air-conditioner has been on the whole time.' Then after a pause he added, 'But it's been three days now. I am doing my best but he's beginning to smell. I must find a way to bury him soon.'

When I hung up I could not write down the account or share it with the other people in the room. I went to the kitchen. I put on the kettle. I looked at the floor tiles and tried to imagine the possibility of breaking them with the hammer that was in the bottom drawer. I was sure the hammer was there. It is not unusual to keep a hammer in the kitchen, I thought. Perhaps the old man too had one in his kitchen drawer. I pictured him hacking away at the masonry until he reached the earth.

10. The Flag

A month later, Izzo and Marwan were amongst a small group of revolutionaries who travelled the 55-kilometre journey from Misrata and slipped into Zliten. There is a video that was shot on Izzo's mobile phone on the 12th of July, which happened to be Marwan's thirtieth birthday. The camera shakes. It stops on a view of marble steps and a wrought-iron balustrade – ornate, copying some distant European staircase. Izzo adjusts the zoom. For a moment his finger is pressed against the glass of the lens. The blood-filled flesh lights up a luminous pink. It reminds me of when, as a child, I used to lock myself in the cupboard and press a torch against my palm, marvelling, with horror and curiosity, at the mysterious web of veins, the opaque sticks of bone. There is the echo of a distant gunshot, then another. Izzo's finger moves out of the frame and we see the ceiling, dotted in a line of spotlights.

'Are you filming?' Marwan whispers.

'Take this,' Izzo tells him and hands him a wooden pole with the red, black and green flag of the revolution.

For a fraction of a second we see Marwan's face, his eyes. He takes the flag in one hand; in the other he is carrying a Kalashnikov. 'Stay close,' Marwan whispers, and begins climbing, two steps at a time. He repeats, 'Stay close.'

'OK, let's do it,' Izzo says, and asks for God's protection.

On every landing there is a wall of brown tinted glass. Several of the panes are smashed. The sun pours through unevenly.

Izzo whispers his commentary: 'We are going up to the roof to take down the dictator's flag,' and asks again for God's protection.

The flagpole now crosses Marwan's back; its new pale wood is fixed behind his belt, and the fabric is above his head, draping over his right shoulder. Izzo reminds him to be vigilant, but Marwan pushes on ahead. Izzo repeats the prayer. The sun has made a polished steel plate of the roof. Marwan leans into the shade of a corner, taps the floor. 'Leave them here,' he whispers, and several similar flagpoles that Izzo had been carrying clank cleanly against the tiles.

Television satellite dishes, as large as elephant ears, are dotted around the rooftop, each pointing in a different direction. There is a water tank. Marwan climbs to the top of it, using an old wooden ladder. The rusty hinges of an old door nearby can be heard. But Marwan doesn't stop to look around. He is moving with the impatient confidence of someone who has not thought a lot about what he is doing. The water tank is just taller than him, and above it two small green flags flutter furiously in the wind.

'The rags of the tyrant,' Izzo whispers.

Marwan snatches the pole of one of the green flags and throws it on the roof tiles.

'Gently,' Izzo tells him. 'Gently, I said.'

But Marwan is already reaching for the second flag. He chucks it down with the same irritated force. He takes up the new flag. Perhaps emboldened by his friend, Izzo continues his commentary but is now no longer whispering. He sounds young.

'God is great,' he says. 'Here is the flag of freedom, the flag of life.' Then he watches silently as Marwan fastens the top of the flagpole to a metal rod above the water tank.

As the red, green and black colours of the flag rise and catch the sun, Marwan shouts, 'God is great,' and Izzo joins him, then adds, 'God bless our country.'

The anxious silence returns as Marwan struggles to tie the pole in place with one hand. More gunshots tear the silence. The wind ripples in loud bass notes against the microphone.

'There is the beautiful flag,' Izzo says softly. 'The flag of life and liberty.' Then, in the manner of a news reporter, he says, 'The freedom fighters of eastern Libya fly the first liberation flag in the town of Zliten.'

The flag is now fixed firmly in place, and reaches at least two metres above the water tank. Marwan checks it, then walks away.

'God bless you,' Izzo tells him.

A broad white smile is carved into Marwan's face.

Izzo laughs quietly. 'Shall I stop filming?' he asks.

'No, carry on,' Marwan tells him, and the two descend the staircase.

At the first landing Marwan stands in front of a flat door and kicks it in. They slowly make their way through the rooms. The furniture is upturned, the curtains ripped.

'See what they've done?' Izzo tells Marwan.

'The dogs,' Marwan says. 'They've trashed the place.'

On the wall of the dining room there are pro-Qaddafi slogans written in red lipstick. Marwan tries to rub them out.

'Here,' Izzo says and hands him the lipstick.

'Let's go,' Marwan says.

'No,' Izzo insists. 'We must write "Libya is Free" and "Down with Qaddafi".'

Marwan begins to write but someone comes in behind them and says, 'Where the hell are you? We have to go. Right now.'

Marwan takes the camera, and for a second Izzo can be seen writing with the lipstick, his back hunched. It reminds me of our grandfather Hamed's back in his latter years.

They exit the building and are in the bright sun. They are moving fast. One of their companions who was guarding the building boasts, 'Did you see them run away?'

'How many were they?' Izzo asks, moving ahead, sounding older now.

'They had two cars,' the other answers.

Marwan asks, 'Were they many?'

In the distance, Izzo can be heard saying, 'They must be hiding over there.'

Marwan points the camera back and you can see the flag high above the water tank. There is no mistaking it.

*

Thirty-eight days later, thirty-eight days into his thirtieth year, on the 19th of August, in a battle in Zliten, Marwan was shot several times in the chest, neck and head. Izzo rushed him to hospital. A few hours later Marwan was photographed lying in a dark green body bag, blood-stained bandages around the top of his head, neck and torso, leaving only the face bare: the skin is clean, the eyes are shut, and the lips open. It cannot be described as an expression but rather as the absence of one. An infinite rest that was always there, behind all of the other faces of his life: the boy sitting proudly by the window on an aeroplane, the young graduate in a suit and tie, the freedom fighter in a beard and red beret, and all the other photographs Marwan's family has posted on the Internet. It makes me think that we all carry, from childhood, our death mask with us.

The two friends had made a promise. If either of them fell, the other would bury the body in the city where they had first met, Misrata. Izzo carried Marwan there, then returned to Zliten and continued the push till the revolutionaries reached Tripoli. On the 23rd of August 2011, they entered the capital. Izzo found his older brother, Hamed, who had joined another rebel unit, waiting for him by the gates of Bab al-Azizia, Qaddafi's compound. They were amongst the first to break into the fortified compound.

'We were convinced,' Hamed told me, 'that we would find Uncle Jaballa there.'

With their comrades, the two brothers reached Qaddafi's house. They found it empty. Izzo located a

weapons depot that gave the rebels access to more ammunition. Feeling secure, they ran across to the next building.
What they didn't know was that a sniper remained on the
roof of that building. He fired a single bullet. It entered
Izzo's forehead and exited from the other side. Izzo fell
on Hamed's shoulder. Hamed tried to stop the bleeding.
The sniper fired again, wounding Hamed in the right leg
and the left lung. But somehow he found the strength to
carry Izzo to safety. A couple of hours later, at 9 p.m.,
Izzo died in hospital. His last words were that he wanted
to be buried beside Marwan. The following morning he
was laid to rest in Misrata.

Uncle Mahmoud called to tell me the news.

'I grieve to be separated from him,' he said.

I felt dizzy. 'It's terrible,' I said.

But Uncle Mahmoud did not call just to inform me of
the bad news. He wanted me to speak to Aunt Zaynab.

'She's losing her mind,' he said. 'Comfort her; tell her
you will do what you can to bring Hamed home.'

Hamed was recovering in a hospital in Misrata, intend-
ing, as soon as he was well enough, to return to Tripoli
and continue fighting. Uncle Mahmoud and Aunt Zaynab
went to try to convince him to return home to Ajdabiya.
He refused and threatened to scream if they tried to force
him. That, due to his wounded lung, the doctor warned,
would kill him.

Hamed recovered and went to the front again. He did
not return to Ajdabiya until Tripoli was liberated. Once
home, he started having a recurring dream. Izzo appears
healthy and content. 'Where I am is much better,' Izzo

tells his brother in the dream. The dream unsettled Hamed. When I visited, I noticed how he hardly slept. He always looked tired. He rarely said much. I asked him once about the war. All he said was, 'You have no idea.' One afternoon, without introduction, he listed for me some of the terrible crimes the Bashar al-Assad regime was committing against the Syrian people. His wounded leg had not recovered properly. He was in pain and had a pronounced limp. An operation needed to be done, but the medical facilities in Libya were poor. He would need to go abroad. A few months after I saw him in Ajdabiya, the health ministry paid for him to go for treatment in Turkey. His flight landed in Istanbul but he did not call home. The surgeon who was going to operate on his leg said Hamed had not turned up at the hospital. For a whole week no one knew where he was. Then Hamed telephoned his father.

'I'm sorry I couldn't call earlier. It took longer than I thought. But I'm now over the border in Syria. I've joined the resistance.'

We all scrambled to try to get him to return. At one point I reached him on the mobile number he had given Uncle Mahmoud. I could not contain my anger.

'This is not resistance,' I shouted down the line. 'It's suicide.'

After a pause he said, very calmly, 'We have to defeat these dictators.'

A few days later he was wounded. His fellow-fighters transported him across the border to a hospital in Turkey. Uncle Mahmoud and Aunt Zaynab flew over to see him.

After a long period of convalescence, Hamed returned with his parents to Ajdabiya.

*

Amongst the photographs Amal has been posting were those taken moments after Izzo died. The blood had been washed off his face, and the place where the bullet entered his skull was bandaged as if there were still hope he might recover. The emergency doctors must have used some disinfectant, or perhaps this is the colour blood stains the skin, because around his right temple and cheekbone Izzo's face is a shade of yellow. It brings to mind the colour of the hot, waxy syrup my aunts cooked up – the smell of burning sugar and orange blossom pulling us children indoors to stick our fingers into the syrup. As soon as it cooled and hardened, the women would spoil it, spreading it in sheets over their arms and legs, snatching quickly and sucking in air from the pain; the sound like fabric tearing. On one occasion cousin Ibtesam – in those days she and I were inseparable – cried, not only upset at their ruining the syrup but also in anticipation of the torture womanhood promised.

'There must be an easier way,' she screamed.

I seconded her opinion.

But we were told categorically that this was the best way, because it plucked the little black hairs right out at the roots. They asked Ibtesam and me to run our fingers on the skin, 'smooth as marble', but inflamed and lacquered a weak shade of yellow.

11. The Last Light

We stood outside Uncle Mahmoud's house in the evening sun and said goodbye. I promised to be back in a few days. I wondered if I was being taken for a shy swimmer who plunges into the river, then gets out immediately. Guilt is exile's eternal companion. It stains every departure. The excuse – for there must always be an excuse – was that I was obliged to visit other relatives in Benghazi. We set off.

The last light stretched long and yet as bright as the skin of a ripe orange. It had been an exceptionally wet winter. Spring was more verdant than anyone could remember, which was taken as an omen for the better future that would surely follow. Greenery thinly covered the desert floor on either side of the road. Feathers of coloured plastic clung to it. Waste wrapped itself around fences and lamp-posts too. Rubbish collection had been practically non-existent since the war. It wasn't until we were out on the open road that the earth shook off the debris and stood as all the unpeopled landscapes of Libya stand, clean and witnessing. The trees, sporadically scattered across the floor of the desert, leant in the direction of the wind, each keeping a distance from the next. They looked as feeble and fragile in the expanse as I remembered them from my childhood, when Father used to drive us from Tripoli to visit his family in Ajdabiya. The twelve-hour journey, from which we all emerged stiff-bodied and tired, seemed part of the dreary effort of making the world monochrome. How colourless this landscape seemed to me then. And now, as much as I resisted disliking a place my father loved, I also enjoyed the familiarity of this old, childish longing for the colours and distractions of the capital and its sea. How odd to enjoy a longing now superseded by other places and the fragile life I had made for myself some 3,000 kilometres north, in a land where none of the words I grew up hearing are spoken, where my grandfather, had he been alive, would not be able to read a word of what I have written, and where the colours contradict, as though deliberately, those of the southern Mediterranean. And, although over time I have grown affectionately accustomed to the palette of London's weather – accustomed but also appreciative of its dour beauty – its colours have remained to me as unnatural as the invisible film placed on windows to dull the light. In the car driving away from Ajdabiya, towards Benghazi and its coast, I realized that I have been carrying within me all these years the child I once was, his particular language and details, his impatient and thirsty teeth wanting to dig into the cold flesh of a watermelon, waking up wondering only about one thing: 'What is the sea like today? Is it flat as oil or ruffled white with the spit of waves?'

*

When we reached Benghazi, I found my cousin Marwan al-Tashani waiting at the hotel. He was sitting at one of the small round tables in the cafeteria, hunched over his laptop, an empty cup of coffee beside him and a cigarette burning between his fingers. He was energized by the positive response his legal NGO was receiving from lawyers and judges across the country. Encouragements and support were also coming in from colleagues in Tunisia, Egypt and Morocco. The revolution had transformed Marwan. He went from being a prosecutor infamous for not being able to get out of bed before noon to one of the most energetic and articulate campaigners for human rights and the importance and inviolability of legal institutions. He saw in the revolution an opportunity to free the courts from political interference. He also wanted to guard due process from revolutionary fervour.

'What do you think?' he said under the noise of the television pinned to the wall high above our heads.

He showed me the logo he had just received from the graphic designer. It had the familiar winding line of the Libyan Mediterranean coast and, towering above it, giant scales. At the bottom there were the words LIBYAN JUDGES' ORGANIZATION written in simple modern type.

As a boy, Marwan was always keen to impress. I remember him as a sensitive child often trying to second-guess the opinions of others. I am a year older and that, back when we were seven and eight, seemed an age. We did not meet again until 1992, when I was twenty-two and Marwan twenty-one. My brother, Ziad, who is only four years my senior, was getting married. The timing coincided with improvements in Libyan–Egyptian relations. The Libyan dictatorship had just lifted restrictions on travel to Egypt, which allowed Marwan and several other relatives to attend the wedding in Cairo. It had then been thirteen years since I had seen my relatives, and two years since we lost Father. I did not tell Mother what time my flight was due to land. I didn't want anyone to pick me up. I needed to compose myself in the taxi ride from the airport. I stood at the door to our flat and, before ringing the bell, listened to the familiar voices, all grown up but the child in each still perceptible. I looked down at my own grown-up leather shoes. They did not seem to belong to me.

During those days surrounding Ziad's wedding, we all fell so completely back into a family again. The past, like a severed limb, tried to fix itself on to the body of the present. Unlike my paternal family, my maternal aunts and cousins were constantly reaching out and touching one another, as though one of us might suddenly disappear. Unlike the austerity of Ajdabiya, where idle talk is suspect, my mother's landscape, the Green Mountains, is verdant with vegetation and talk. I remember how, when we used to drive there, the green landscape would gradually take over and the earth would rise. Mountains would suddenly enclose us. Looking down, I would occasionally spot a stream or waterfall. Then eventually the twisting road would release us at the open sea. In this region, light and shade were not definite, as they were in Ajdabiya, but moved with the leaves and the breeze. Conversation here too, or at least amongst my maternal family, reflected this variety. They had an exceptional gift for gossip, a good memory for songs, took delight in conversation and knew how to enjoy themselves. It made leaving them in Cairo very difficult.

On the flight back to London after the wedding, I tried to keep awake. I was flying KLM, stopping briefly at Amsterdam before continuing on to London. The plane was full of Dutch families. But, even with eyes wide open, I remained convinced that they were all speaking Arabic and in an accent more authentically Libyan than my own. I felt the shadows of my aunts' and cousins' hands, now round my wrist, tapping my shoulder, through my hair, then with a feathery touch brushing my ankle. I was twenty-two and my small London flat was crowded with old questions, more severe now than ever.

In the early 1990s, after the border was opened, no one visited Mother in Cairo more frequently than Marwan. I would often see him during my holidays there. A distance had grown between us, and not only because of our time apart. Like the rest of my cousins, Marwan had endured the restrictions and interferences of Qaddafi's Libya. He had witnessed the militarization of schools, where, as a young boy, he had to turn up in military uniform and crawl on the ground with a rifle before morning class. He had seen the banning of books, music and films, the closure of theatres and cinemas, the outlawing of football, and all the other countless ways in which the Libyan dictatorship, like a crazed jealous lover, infiltrated every aspect of public and private life. He had a certain air of unease, fortified by both pride and anxiety.

Over dinner at our house, if someone criticized the dictator, Marwan would fall silent or leave the room. I understood why. We all knew of people who had been arrested only because they were present when the dictatorship had been criticized. Nonetheless, it created a fog between us. I wanted him to condemn the regime. Every time my eyes fell on Father's portrait in the dining room, my heart grew small and hard. I was an angry young man then. We tiptoed around each other, trying our best to avoid confronting the ways in which political reality manages to infiltrate intimacies, corrupting them with unuttered longings and accusations.

In January 2011, as the Libyan dictatorship attempted to prevent the kind of uprisings seen in Tunisia and Egypt, not only did the regime free political prisoners, such as my uncles and cousins, but it also promised interest-free loans to young people and a dramatic increase in foreign scholarships for university students. This was happening in tandem with violent crackdowns on journalists and human rights activists. Fathi Terbil, a lawyer who had represented the relatives of over one thousand political prisoners killed in Abu Salim prison, was arrested. It was in response to this that on the night of the 15th of February 2011, two days before the planned beginning of the Libyan revolution, Marwan, together with a dozen or so judges and lawyers, staged a protest that even they at the time saw as nothing more than a symbolic gesture. They stood on the steps of the Benghazi courthouse, where, many years before, when Marwan's father, Sidi Ahmed, was the High Court judge, Marwan, his brother, Nafa, and I used to run up and down the corridors, thrilled by the need to keep quiet, making sure the tennis ball we threw from one end to the other did not knock against any of the closed doors. I called Marwan that evening, as he stood with the others on the steps of the courthouse in the cold winter breeze, with the sea, invisible in the night, murmuring in the background.

'Can you hear it?' he said, and I pictured him holding the mobile phone up towards the mass of black water.

'All good courthouses should face the sea,' I told him.

'Exactly,' he said, laughing. 'This way there is nowhere to run.'

The following night, the evening of the 16th of February, Marwan and his colleagues took their places again in front of the courthouse.

'It was like stepping off a cliff,' he said. 'It was more frightening than the first night. We heard what they had done to demonstrators in Al-Bayda and elsewhere.'

That night, the lawyers and judges expected a crackdown. Instead, what emerged through the surrounding dark streets were the families of the deceased, those whose cases Fathi Terbil had taken on. Hundreds of people came, and the following day the numbers grew into the thousands. On the 17th of February, the date after which the revolution was named, the authorities attacked and killed several demonstrators. Instead of scaring people away, it had the opposite effect. I called Marwan. He sounded as if he had been arguing. His wife had been trying to convince him to stay at home.

'She said, "Aren't you frightened for your daughter?" I told her, "It is exactly because I am afraid for my daughter's future that I am going out."'

Revolutions have their momentum, and once you join the current it is very difficult to escape the rapids. Revolutions are not solid gates through which nations pass but a force comparable to a storm that sweeps all before it. One of Turgenev's most affecting characters does not come from his best-known novels. Alexey Dmitrievich Nezhdanov, the hero of *Virgin Soil*, Turgenev's last novel, is the illegitimate son of an aristocrat. He is young and trapped between two powerful impulses: a romantic sensibility that makes him ill-suited for absolute certainty, and a revolutionary heart that craves that certainty. These opposing forces in his nature eventually destroy him. Nezhdanov has always interested me, and now it seemed Marwan and I and nearly everyone we knew were falling into a similar predicament.

*

Marwan took me to meet the author and editor Ahmed al-Faitouri. In the early days of the revolution, Ahmed had got my number from a mutual acquaintance and called me in London. He had wanted to revive *Al-Haqiqah*, a newspaper that Qaddafi closed back in the early 1970s. To writers of Ahmed's generation, born in the 1950s and '60s, *Al-Haqiqah* was a valued source of independent news and high literary discourse. When he could not acquire the name from the publisher, he set up *Al-Mayadin* instead. The name means 'squares'. He wanted to call it that because, he had explained over the telephone, 'the revolutions in Tunisia, Egypt and here all broke out from public squares'. The mission of *Al-Mayadin* was to 'document the 17 February revolution at the political, economic, social, cultural and judicial levels'. He was obviously a man of great energy and ability, because, in the midst of the fighting and instability of the time, he managed to bring out the first issue three months after the revolution started, when the regime was yet to fall. He was not alone. Libyan journalism, that frail and battered institution, was experiencing a resurgence at the time. For four decades under Qaddafi, journalists were censored, imprisoned and sometimes killed. In the few months after the uprising, Libya went from producing a handful of government-administered periodicals to up to 200 newspapers, magazines and leaflets. Running short of space, newsagents began spreading out the periodicals on the pavement in front of their shops. Most of the publications were amateur, but they expressed the country's appetite for a free and plural press. Leafing through them, you sensed the urgency not only to monitor the evolving present but also to engage in the past, publishing accounts and personal testimonies of life under the dictatorship. When Ahmed al-Faitouri telephoned in 2011, he did not do so just to tell me of his dream, 'a dream that had been, up to now, a sin', but to persuade me to write for *Al-Mayadin*, 'on any subject: politics, literature, art, anything'. I did not need much convincing. Until then, my books and journalism had been banned in Libya. I vividly remember the day when I discovered that the authorities had censored my work and had even forbidden editors from printing my name. It was in July 2006, a month after the publication of my first novel. I had just given a reading at the Poetry Café on Betterton Street in Covent Garden and, hoping to calm my nerves, I went outside to smoke. A man stepped out of the café behind me. He turned out to be a Libyan journalist living in London. He freelanced for several of the main publications and had been looking forward to writing a review of my novel. When he told his editor in Tripoli of his plan, the editor responded, 'Please, nothing on Hisham Matar. We have direct orders.' But my book had already been smuggled into the country by then. Photocopies were made and circulated. My articles were also translated, often without my knowledge, and posted on the Internet.

'Apart from a few literary people, nobody knows you here,' Marwan said, driving me to Ahmed's house. 'I have decided to become your Libya publicist.' He had been telephoning journalists, letting them know I had returned.

'I am here to see my family. I don't want to give interviews.'

'That's your problem,' he said, the steering wheel competing with a cigarette in one hand and a mobile phone in the other.

The tree-lined street was narrow and quiet. Most of the houses on it were designed in the Italian style of the early 1900s: symmetric, plain, single-storey structures. Only occasionally an ornamental, classical detail was allowed: a painted frieze or an ornate modillion propping up a cornice. Above the door to Ahmed's house, there was the faded triangle of a painted pediment. Beyond the large, modest, tiled entrance, the house was made up of two identical flats. Ahmed and his wife lived in one, and the other was dedicated to the newspaper's editorial office and, in the evenings, to literary gatherings. Walking us through, Ahmed said, 'Back in the 1920s and '30s, the house served as the residence of the head of the Italian Fascist Party in Benghazi.'

We sat in the editorial office. The walls were lined with books. A portrait of Ahmed Rafiq al-Mahdawi rested on one shelf, looking young and determined, resembling less the national poet that he was and more a doubting author. Under the Italian occupation, al-Mahdawi was forced to flee to Turkey. After independence, he returned and was appointed by King Idris to the senate. He became the centre of the literary and cultural life of the country. It was said that in the afternoons he could always be found at Benghazi's Arrudi Café, which used to be on the corner of Baladiya Square, in the heart of the city. Young writers, artists and intellectuals of the day – figures such as Mohammad Faraj Hemmi, the leftist academic and lawyer who was later arrested by Qaddafi and died under torture in prison in 1981, and Basili Shafik Khouzam, the author who would later chronicle life in Benghazi in a series of novels and short stories written in Italian under the pen name of Alessandro Spina – frequented Arrudi, drawn to al-Mahdawi's table. Some of the names I spotted on Ahmed's shelves were William Faulkner and Ernest Hemingway, Italo Calvino and Albert Camus, Milan Kundera and Mario Vargas Llosa.

'Finally, things can happen,' Ahmed said when he saw me glance at his bookshelf. 'You'll find holes, no doubt.

But you can't imagine the acrobatics, the sheer acrobatics we had to go through to get our hands on these books. And then once you do, and the word gets around, friends come asking to borrow them. You try to build a library, but neither the censor nor the people will let you!' he said and laughed.

I asked him if before the revolution he had been anxious that the authorities would find out he owned these books.

'No, the decision to ban certain books was never taken out of passion – I wish it had been. It was just out of indifference and spite. A sort of natural reflex.'

The problem was not only the censor, Ahmed explained; the regime's repeated assaults on bookshops – confiscating their stock and closing some of them down – meant that it was practically very difficult to find books in Libya, even those the censor had permitted. I knew this because the oldest and most reputable Libyan publisher and bookseller, Al-Fergiani, eventually had to move its offices to London.

Ahmed smoked incessantly, which worried me because whenever he laughed, which was frequently, his face would fill up with blood and he would lose his breath. I warmed to him. He had a cheerful disposition and, notwithstanding his conclusion that 'Libya has perfected the dark art of devaluing books,' he was an optimist and a tireless advocate for literature and the life of the mind. To be a Libyan artist in Libya was heroic. The country, its politics and social dogmas, thwart every possible artistic instinct. The perseverance of men like Ahmed is astonishing. In 1978, when he was in his early twenties, he was amongst the large group of authors who were incarcerated. The regime had set up a trap. It invited young literary talent to take part in a book festival, then arrested them. Like most of that group, Ahmed spent ten years in prison.

'Qaddafi thought he was hurting me,' he said. 'Instead, he gave me dozens of writer friends. I now have a house in every village and town across the country.'

After a silence, he said, 'Everything is set for your event. It will take place in two days.'

'But that's not possible,' I said. 'I don't want to do public events. I am here to visit my family.'

'It's your family who wants you to do it,' Marwan put in, laughing.

'Why don't we have an evening here, something small, with other writers?' I suggested.

'We have already printed posters,' Ahmed said. 'The conference room in the library has been booked.'

Marwan found the whole thing hilarious. 'You are stuck,' he said as we walked away from Ahmed's house. Then, with pride, he added, 'Nothing ever happens here. But when it does, it happens at the speed of lightning. You can change the world in a day. It might take forty-two years for that day to come, but when it does …'

12. Benghazi

The following day I met more relations. It was odd to be with people I half remembered. At the least-expected moment, I would suddenly recognize the shape of a neck, an expression in the eyes, an intonation in the voice. Somebody would be telling an anecdote and midway through I would realize I had heard it before. It seemed as if everyone else's development had been linear, allowed to progress naturally in the known environment, and therefore each of them seemed to have remained linked, even if begrudgingly or in disagreement, to the original setting-off point. At times I was experiencing a kind of distance-sickness, a state in which not only the ground was unsteady but also time and space. The only other individuals I met who seemed afflicted by a similar condition were ex-prisoners.

> I would never be part of anything. I would never really belong anywhere, and I knew it, and all my life would be the same, trying to belong, and failing. Always something would go wrong. I am a stranger and I always will be, and after all I didn't really care.

When I first read those lines by Jean Rhys, I thought, yes, and then almost immediately resented the connection I felt. This is why returning to that pre-life is like catching your reflection in a public place. Your first reaction, before you realize it is you, is suspicion. You lose your footing but just in time regain your balance. I realize now that my walks, whether taken to pass the time or to better acquaint myself with a foreign city, or conducted in a hurry – to post a letter, to catch a train or on the occasion I was late for an appointment – all took place under the vague suspicion that I might somehow come upon myself, that is to say, that other self who lives in harmony with his surroundings, who exists, like a chapter in a book, in the right place, not torn out and left to make sense on its own.

All the tools I had to connect with my country belonged to the past. Rage, like a poisoned river, had been running through my life ever since we left Libya. It made itself into my anatomy, into the details. Grief as a virus. But now I could see the walls, so old I had never noticed them before, that stood between me and everyone I have ever known, every book and painting and symphony and work of art that had ever mattered to me, suddenly seeming impermanent. The freedom frightened me – because, after all, as a man, I felt made. I wandered through the streets of Benghazi. The city had always been unenthusiastic about the Qaddafi regime, and it paid the price. The neglect here had an air of punishment about it. I left the waterfront and entered the maze of the old downtown, through Omar al-Mukhtar Street, under the shade of its colonnade, turning into narrow lanes that led to quiet, dead-end squares where, I imagined, even with the windows open at midday, one could feel calm enough to work. All along I was churned up by the new possibility of making this city my home. I was both thrilled and resistant. Perhaps my choice to enter Libya through Benghazi, I now thought, was not as accidental as I had assumed. Although we had lived in Tripoli and my mother was from Derna and my father from Ajdabiya, Benghazi, at least today, seemed to belong to me alone. I met Diana at the Café Vittoria by the water. We relished the chance to be away from others. I secretly began to imagine us shipping our books and pictures and music here. Packing them all on a container headed for this city by the sea, a city made for things to arrive.

Downtown Benghazi runs in an L-shape along the water. The longer stretch faces due north. The locals refer to this side as the Arabic Corniche. If the wind is good, you could be in Crete in a day. The square tower of the lighthouse is set peculiarly back, as if shy of the sea, or not shy at all but beckoning, daring the Mediterranean to come closer. Scattered about it are the remains of several buried cities: a Greek wall that dates back some 2,300 years, ruins from a Roman settlement, a Byzantine church, and, I am sure, if excavations were conducted, clues to Phoenician life would be found too. From here the living city begins, the houses and markets of the medieval Arabic city together with what the Ottomans added. But what dominates is the present, the low-rise concrete blocks with their antennae and satellite dishes. Benghazi, more than most cities, is a contested space, a city in the making, a city open to interpretation. A few months from now, that energy that was expressing itself in unbounded hope and optimism would turn darkly on itself, seeking expression in blood and carnage.

Café Vittoria is on the other side of the L, what the old folk used to call the Lungomare – 'seafront' in Italian – and now everyone refers to as the Italian Corniche. The café occupies the spot where Mussolini landed. Lest Il Duce's eyes be offended, a great deal of trouble went into erasing any signs that this was an Arab and Muslim city. Not one Ottoman or Arab minaret, house, colonnade or dome could be seen from this angle. It was a feat of architectural camouflage. Indeed, the neoclassical buildings that line the seafront are so basic that they could almost be part of a film set, albeit an old and decrepit one. Punctuating this Italian disguise is the Benghazi cathedral, one of the largest Roman Catholic churches in North Africa. It hovers at the water's edge, as though looking for direction, its twin domes naked of crosses.

On the 7th of April 1977, as a response to the student union's demand to protect the academy from growing political interference, two students, Omar Ali Dabboub and Mohammad bin Saud, were hanged in the gardens of the cathedral. On the 7th of April 1992, when I was an architecture student in London, and more out of boredom and curiosity than a conscious desire to commemorate the fifteenth anniversary of the event, I spent a few hours in the library, looking into the life of the architect who designed the cathedral. Guido Ferrazza, it turned out, had had an eventful life. He was born a long way away from Benghazi, in a small Alpine village near Trento. The name of the town is Bocenago, and, not long after that afternoon in my university library, I found myself wandering through the streets of Bocenago. Its population when I visited barely exceeded 300. Back in 1887, the year Guido Ferrazza was born, it was double that size. Mountains rose up around the town from all sides. The snow and rock and greenery made the sky seem unusually enormous and close. The sun was out. The light did not seem to shine down on the valley as much as pour in and fill it like liquid. As I walked through the village streets, all the buildings seemed empty. From here, Ferrazza went to university in Milan. He was obviously afflicted with restlessness. On graduating, he went abroad to Bulgaria, where he consulted on works on the St Alexander Nevsky cathedral in Sofia, and then on to far-off Singapore and Bangkok, where he worked on the royal residence. He project-managed numerous construction sites in South America and seemed to be considering settling there. He worked on the parliament of Montevideo, a monumental structure designed by Vittorio Meano. I imagine Ferrazza saw a role model in Vittorio Meano. He was a generation older, had also come from a small village in the far north of Italy, and was now heading a successful architectural practice in Argentina. On completing the work in Montevideo, Ferrazza returned with his mentor to Buenos Aires. But a great misfortune was awaiting Vittorio Meano. On arriving home, he found his wife in bed with another man. Witnesses heard a gunshot, and then the voice of the architect shouting, 'They murdered me!' Soon after this, Ferrazza returned to Italy.

In 1927, when Ferrazza was forty, Attilio Teruzzi, the

then governor of Cyrenaica, called him to prepare a new plan for Benghazi. Teruzzi was not an indifferent bureaucrat; in 1922, as one of the commanders of the Blackshirts, he had taken part in the Fascists' March on Rome. Libya offered Ferrazza a golden opportunity to implement his ideas. It launched him as a major architect in the colonies. Under his supervision, Benghazi was to become a new Italian city. He moved there and began work immediately. The project kept him so busy that when, a couple of years later and on account of his success in Benghazi, he was asked to produce plans for the capital, Tripoli, he accepted but delegated the new commission to his partners. A few years later, in 1935, he moved to Eritrea, where he was appointed chief architect of Asmara. Later he would design entire districts of Harrar and Addis Ababa.

But a unique architectural expression had occurred in Benghazi, or Bengasi Italiana, as the city's Italian inhabitants – who numbered, in Ferrazza's time, about one-third of the population – referred to it then. Whereas the colonial architecture in Tripoli is sober and decidedly neoclassical – there are streets in Tripoli where you could very well be in Italy – in Benghazi you can always see the crossroads and the layers. The cocktail of influences – Arab, Ottoman, Italianate, European modernist – suits the relaxed, eclectic and rebellious nature of the city. But there is something else, a material that does not belong to any other culture or period. It is timeless and unique to Benghazi. It is perhaps the most important architectural material there is, more than stone. It is light. The Benghazi light is a material. You can almost feel its weight, the way it falls and holds its subject.

Even from this distance, after all the neglect and poor planning that had followed, I could see what excitement men such as Ferrazza must have felt here: the superior optimism, at once reckless and misguided, that pulsed through him and his Milanese contemporaries as they paced up and down the Benghazi waterfront, turning Africa, as an Italian colonel in one of Alessandro Spina's novels puts it, 'into a bordello and offering her up to our young men, so that they may vent the entire spectrum of their human, heroic, sadistic and aesthetic emotions'.

In July 1943, as Italy was being devastated in the war, Ferrazza showed a great instinct for self-preservation and moved to England. He joined the exiled resistance there. This is how, in 1945, when the Fascist regime disintegrated completely and Attilio Teruzzi – the man who had first brought Ferrazza to Benghazi – was fleeing south from the Partisans, Ferrazza was granted an honourable return to his country. For the next four years, he served on numerous committees charged with post-war reconstruction. In the spring of 1949, in a sudden yearning for adventure, or perhaps wanting to emulate his unfortunate mentor, Vittorio Meano, Ferrazza decided to emigrate to Argentina. There was no clear reason why, two years later, he returned to Milan. He lived a quiet retirement until, on the 1st of February 1961, perhaps out of nostalgia that in old age seemed inescapable, Guido Ferrazza boarded a train for Bocenago, his birthplace in the Alps. The carriage he was in derailed and crashed a few kilometres outside Milan. He was seventy-four.

Sitting with Diana at Café Vittoria, where we had a good view of the water, the length of the corniche and the cathedral, I tried to imagine Guido Ferrazza's face. As hard as I tried, I could not find a photograph of him in my university library. Perhaps my old theory that saw connections between the façades of buildings and the faces of their architects was not entirely ridiculous. Judging from the over-earnest symmetry of the Benghazi cathedral, I pictured a face imprinted with a similar expression of uncertain confidence, unmoored by history and rather large and awkward, doing its best not to engage too much in introspection, peering instead into the distance with searching yet somewhat wary eyes.

We drank our coffee and talked about living here part of the year. The light was slowly seeping out of the sky. The sea was calm but not still. Its surface was mapped with current lines running in different directions, as faint as sleep marks on skin. I felt I was not observing but remembering, as if Diana and I had already lived here and were now returning in the same spirit in which we had visited other cities where we had once lived, standing together in front of a building we used to call home and feeling that odd sensation one feels when the changes in us are juxtaposed against the constancy of a familiar geography. In the background of these thoughts, I could detect an echo of an old power: that childhood conviction that the Libyan sea was an open door and that appetite for an authentic acquaintance with nature, which had become less consistent over the years, was returning now unhindered, renewed. I don't mean a casual desire for travel, not a tourist's curiosity for sites and landmarks and languages and new faces, but a precise and uncomplicated conviction that the world was available to me. But wasn't this an odd thing to think now, now that I was finally home? Or is this what being home is like: home as a place from which the entire world is suddenly possible?

*

The following morning, Maher Bushrayda, a cousin I had not seen or spoken to since I had left Libya as a child, dropped by. Maher is a generation older than me, and I only vaguely recall his visits to us in Tripoli. He seemed cool and mysterious to me then, probably because he was a member of the student union at Benghazi University. He took part in the demonstration in 1976. A year later, when Omar Ali Dabboub and Mohammad bin Saud, who were close friends of his, were hanged, Maher, along with several other students, was arrested and spent the years from 1977 to 1986 in prison. He was the first in our family to face the consequences of criticizing the dictatorship, and this, in the years after we left Libya, lent him, in my naive teenage mind, a romantic mystique. We had met the day before, at a large family gathering, and set a time to speak privately. We had coffee in my hotel. He confirmed what he had told me yesterday, that he had joined the new secret service, which was, in his words, 'scrambling to fill the gap'.

His two chief concerns, he said, were 'security and the opportunists', the armed groups vying for power.

'What of the Islamists?' I asked.

'They won't succeed,' Maher said, and then proceeded to tell me about a Tunisian rapper who, having been threatened by an Islamic group, was forced to cancel a planned concert. 'These people want a country without art, without conferences, without cinemas. An empty hole,' he said.

'And they succeeded with the Tunisian,' I said.

'Yes, but it's a failed policy.'

Eventually the conversation turned to the main purpose of our meeting: how, in his new position, he might help me find out what had happened to my father. Maher had his shirtsleeves rolled up, his elbows resting on the table. He pinched his flesh hard and spoke softly.

'Uncle Jaballa is in my skin. I was very close to him. You were young; you might not remember.' Then he went to that place I was meant to have become accustomed to, where, through veiled speech, I was to understand the obvious, that my father was dead.

'I have no doubt about that,' I lied. 'What we want to find out is how and when it happened, where the body might be.'

A strange thing happened then, something that had never occurred before. I sensed my father's presence, just behind my right shoulder, beckoning me away, and I expected him to say – somehow I knew it was on the tip of his tongue – 'Stop. Enough now.'

I couldn't move or speak. Thankfully, Maher stood up

and said he had to go. I walked him out, watched him skip over the puddle that was always at the base of the steps outside the hotel. I recognized his prison body. That slightly stifled gait all political prisoners have. As though oppression were toxic sediment that lingered in the muscles. It expressed itself in a certain reticence. And the grievance seemed not to be with fate or ideology but with humanity itself. I waved as he drove off. He held his thumb up in a good-luck sign. I remembered his last words: 'I'm here for you till the end of time. Anything you need. As for the hereafter,' he said, and laughed, 'you are on your own.'

*

I went for a walk by the seafront. A plump boy, who was ten at most, rode a large quad bike through the families. Some sat on the low wall looking out at the sea, others had their backs to it, preferring instead to watch the promenade. The water was calm, reflecting the sky. Beyond the rocks that separated the shallow from the deep, the waters were massive but unthreatening, waiting, certain. The plump boy was doing circles now, the two front wheels up in the air. He almost ran into a couple. They, and he, seemed unperturbed. Now, with the front wheels still about a foot above the tiled ground, he headed straight towards one of the bollards that had clearly been placed at such intervals along the promenade to stop exactly this sort of thing. He slowed down, tightened the turn and threaded through, showing exceptional control. He stopped, as if expecting the applause he so rightly deserved. An even younger boy ran up to him and hopped on to the back of the quad bike. They sped off. A young boy and girl were playing football with paper cups. The father said, 'What are you doing?' 'Playing,' the girl answered, but she had stopped playing and was facing him. 'Playing with rubbish?' the father asked. 'There is nothing else to play with,' the boy told him and pulled the girl. A few steps ahead a small child started crying. She buried herself in her father's lap. 'Don't be afraid,' he told her. 'Stop being so frightened of everything.' The two boys on the quad bike flew past, gaining speed. I turned back. Children were running along the pavement. The brother and sister who were playing football with paper cups were now looking out to sea and counting aloud. They came to the end of their numbers and immediately burst out laughing when they caught sight of a small boy hiding behind one of the bollards.

13. Another Life

Word of the event got around. The car park surrounding the library was almost full by the time Mother, Diana and I arrived. The building had the air of an abandoned structure. The floor of the car park was covered in the tiles so commonly found in the southern Mediterranean, made up of broken pieces of marble and other stones set in resin. It was the wrong choice. It was designed for interiors. The relentless assault of the sun and the weight of the cars had cracked it in several places. Weeds and grass shot through the gaps. Up a few steps and we were inside the foyer. There wasn't a book in sight, and even the index-card drawers were empty. I wasn't able to go up to the other floors, but, judging from the ground floor, the library had been empty and closed for years. The vertical blinds that hung against the windows were bent out of shape and several of their long strips were missing.

Elderly men, dressed in suits and ties, stood in a cluster, talking to one another. One of them called to me and, as I approached, without knowing who they were individually, I knew they were my father's friends. This is how old he would be today, I thought. I extended a hand to the first. He pulled me into an embrace. I could feel him shudder. His cheeks were closely shaven. Each one smelt clean and of eau de cologne. I don't remember them saying much at all.

More people began to arrive.

At the opposite end of the foyer, a man, perhaps a decade older than me, held my mother's hand to his chest, and she smiled, clearly happy to see him.

I met men and women my age who knew me from school or summer holidays. They kept asking, 'But really, you don't remember?' Eventually I said, 'You all grew up together. You saw how his face changed and you saw how her body developed. Whereas I haven't seen you in thirty-three years. Of course I don't remember.' It wasn't so much what I said but how I said it that gave me away.

Diana was at the other end of the foyer, surrounded by several of my cousins.

A butterfly had become trapped between the vertical blinds and the glass. The windows had not been washed in a very long time. I imagined scrubbing them down, one after the other, until they were clear. I kept looking to see if the butterfly had broken free, but it remained fluttering, unable to find the opening between the strips.

Although the library seemed ransacked and unused, its conference room was entirely new. The seats were in white leather and the walls panelled in wood. Obviously, meetings had been more important than books. A man about the age of my father was sitting in the front row. He looked at me intently but with soft eyes that were slightly red and seemed to be brimming with tears. On his lap lay a fat leather-bound book. His hands rested on it, trembling a little. I wasn't sure if it was due to emotion or old age. The room was full, all the seats were taken, and several people stood at the back. But because this man was sitting in the front row, we shared a strange intimacy, as I was the only one who could see his expression and therefore it seemed intended for me alone.

Marwan had taken his role as my 'Libya publicist' too seriously. He had produced a slide show. The houselights went down, and the film ran for more than five minutes, showing pictures of Grandfather Hamed, my father, Izzo, and then me and my books, accompanied by a recording of Naseer Shamma playing the oud. The audience sat through it in complete silence. Then the event commenced: a conversation between Ahmed al-Faitouri and me, with my cousin Nafa al-Tashani sitting beside me in case I needed a translator. Although I am fluent in Arabic, I am not used to delivering public talks in it. The event lasted three hours and, halfway through, we had to stop for an intermission.

The old man in the front row stood up and walked over to me. We shook hands. It was clearly difficult for him to speak.

'I was Jaballa's friend,' he said. 'We went to college together.' He handed me the volume he had been holding on to. 'He and I edited the literary journal,' he said.

The man's son, who was one of those trying to remind me earlier of summers we had spent together, said, 'These are the complete issues. I had them bound in one volume.'

I opened it. *The Scholar*, it said, was a literary journal for short fiction. The cover of the June 1957 issue, when my father was eighteen, had an illustration of a stack of

books, an inkwell, a beaming light and a semicircular pro-
tractor. The first page described the publication as 'A
journal published by the students of the Teachers' College of Cyrenaica'. The journal's motto was: 'Education
gains the nation its dignity, sovereignty and pride. Where
knowledge spreads, prosperity, happiness and security
prevail. Education is as necessary as water and oxygen.'
This was the sentiment of the time. Libya was trying to
drag itself into modernity. The policy of the Italian colonial government did not promote education for the
'indigenous' population. Libya's oldest university was not
established until 1955 – only two years before this issue of
The Scholar was published – by royal decree by King Idris
to commemorate the fourth anniversary of independence. Oil was yet to be discovered. Probably because of
its association with literacy, the Faculty of Literature was
the first to be established. Even such a modest start had to
rely on foreign donations. Egypt contributed four lectur-
ers, covering their salaries for four years, and the United
States paid the wages of the Iraqi scholar Majid Khadduri,
who eventually became dean. A year later, in 1956, the
Faculty of Science was established; Economics in 1957;
Law in 1962; Agriculture in 1966; and Medicine in 1970.
This explains the earnest motto of the journal. My father
was one of its three editors, who clearly saw the art of
fiction as part of the national effort to drive up literacy
and education.

I tried to glance through it, but then the old man
returned me to the contents page. Somehow my eyes
couldn't focus. With a gently quivering finger he pointed

to two short stories. The author's name: 'Jaballa Matar'. I knew of my father's attempts at poetry but I had no idea that when he was a student he had fancied himself a writer of prose fiction. My mother was standing beside me by now, looking at the book.

'Did you know about this?'

'I had no idea.'

We turned to the stories. Father's photograph was included. He was wearing a suit and tie and a confidently serious expression. He looked like a young Albert Camus.

One of the stories was called 'In the Stillness of the Night: A Libyan Tale', and the other 'A Struggle with Fate'.

I asked Mother again, 'Are you sure he never mentioned it?'

'No, not a word.'

We decided to open the second half of the event with a reading of 'In the Stillness of the Night'. My cousin Nafa stood up and read:

The wind roared against the tent that stood alone in the desert. Its pegs were firmly planted in the sand. The time was midnight. Darkness perched over the world. The moon, having just taken off its deep red garment, passed now, stretching through the spacious skies. Stillness spread its curtain over everything. The only sounds that could be heard were those of the grazing camels and the lazy melody of the sheep's bleating. Wonderment dominated the universe. Fear had rooted itself into the lives of those who inhabited these parts. Everyone was afraid except the men in the tent: Ahmed, who was his mother's only son, and his maternal uncle. Accompanying them was the uncle's family. Despite the spectre of the enemy, who threatened everyone on this land, Ahmed and his uncle had ventured out to these plains to tend to their livestock. Nothing mattered to them more than the well-being of their flock. Fear was kept at bay because they had sufficient weapons and ammunition, which, on a previous confrontation, they had captured from the enemy.

The 'enemy' was the Italian army unit that was sneaking into the camp to steal the livestock. 'The enemy's eyes,' we are told, 'never sleep.' Once surrounded, the uncle, who is an old man:

> hears inside his chest the defiant cry of a young rebel. He is transformed, feels a bitter strength, and is emboldened by a youthful vigour that, at any moment, is liable to fade, and self-discipline earned by old age and a harsh life … 'No, I will not escape!' he murmured to himself. 'I will not try to escape … I will remain until this white hair is soaked in blood, deep red blood that will spring out of the countless wrinkles in my skin. I will not let disgrace stain my forehead. Let the resistance begin.'

The old man and his nephew bravely defeat the 'Italian invaders'. But then Ahmed cannot find Aisha, his beloved cousin:

[He] was terrified, his muscles contracted and his heart trembled with confusion and anxiety. He was filled with dismal foreboding that one of those evil men had sneaked into the tent and kidnapped her. Ahmed hastened to track the remaining enemy troops, but the old man pulled him by the cloak. Aisha was approaching. With the eagerness of a thirsty man, Ahmed rushed to her. 'Where have you been? What were you doing?' he said with gentle admonition. But he understood everything from her face and the weapon on her shoulder. Nonetheless, he went on asking: 'What is this in your hand?' With the pride of the girls of the African continent, she replied: 'This is a medal I found on the chest of the commandant whom I killed with my own hands.' Ahmed was about to embrace her, but his uncle's presence stopped him.

The story was signed, 'Jaballa Matar, Year 3'. The old man's words, 'I will not let disgrace stain my forehead', were echoed thirty-six years later in Father's first letter from prison, when he wrote, 'My forehead does not know how to bow.' When my father was kidnapped, I was nearly the same age as he was when he wrote this story. Outside of school, I read only poetry. I had only begun to read fiction in my spare time when I was nineteen – in fact, a few days after I had lost my father.

Towards the end of the event, the audience asked questions concerning the challenges the country was facing after the revolution, the place of literature and ideas in Libya, the role of education and civil society, human rights and the importance of addressing past atrocities. 'So we make sure they never happen again.' I answered these, albeit inadequately, but that was not the point somehow. That these questions could be asked in a civil and well-organized literary event was the main objective. As much as I am by nature uneasy about such attention, I knew that any feelings of pride or optimism that I might have provoked in those present that day were in truth not about me at all but, put simply, about the possibility of a different reality, one that we had all glimpsed during the short window of hope between the revolution and the devastation of the civil war that followed. Several of the people that stood up to speak did not ask a question but wanted to tell the gathering a piece of information about my grandfather or father. It was as if I were a stowaway being claimed back by the fatherland. The thirty-three years that troubled me troubled them too. Once these sentiments died down, the man I had seen earlier, who grasped my mother's hand in the foyer, stood up to speak.

'Good evening. I am very happy to take part in celebrating Hisham Matar and his work. I have to be honest, though. I regrettably have not had a chance to read Hisham's books, but I am familiar, of course, with his father's long resistance and the ultimate sacrifice that man made to his country. However, what people here might not know about, and what has not been mentioned this evening, are the silent sacrifices of Hisham's mother, Fawzia Tarbah.'

My mother was sitting in the front row beside Diana. She seemed uncomfortable. She looked at me. She whispered something to Diana, and then they held hands. I think every child is born with a tiny device implanted in their chest that signals the moment their mother is about to cry.

'In the 1970s I took part in the university student protest here in Benghazi,' the man went on. 'I was arrested, taken to a prison in Tripoli. My mother – I'm her only child – was losing her mind. She asked who she could stay with in Tripoli and people told her of a woman who put up mothers of political prisoners. She was known for having an open house to these mothers who travelled the distance to visit their children. I never met this woman, because by the time I was released they told me she had left the country. But my mother, who passed away recently or else she would be here speaking these words, told me about the kind woman in Tripoli. She spent months in her house. And this woman, my mother told me, thought of a thousand tricks to distract my mother. Every week the two women cooked for the entire prison wing, 150 men. They sent us platefuls of the finest food. They sent books, pens and writing pads. The guards stole much, but much also reached us, and what reached us was enough.'

The moment he finished speaking that last line, my mother covered her face.

'We all know what Jaballa Matar did. But I came here tonight not so much for Jaballa or Hisham, but to tell you all what I know of this gracious woman and to thank her, although no amount of gratitude would be sufficient.'

Everyone stood up. When eventually the clapping stopped, the only words my mother could muster, barely audible, were 'Thank you.'

*

Later that evening, back at the hotel, I asked Mother if it was true that she had housed mothers of prisoners.

'Yes, but he exaggerated a little,' she said. 'I did it a couple of times.'

'Obviously enough times that you earned a reputation for it,' I said.

'To be honest, I don't remember. It all seems so long ago. Another life.'

14. The Bullet

The days complicated my nights. I lay in bed turning. It often took several hours to fall asleep. A truth seemed to rise up in the dark. The noises of Benghazi, the sea murmuring beyond, came through the window as though they were solid physical shapes. The night had turned the city into an idea whose sounds were as material as bread and stone. I had never been anywhere so burdened with memories yet also so charged with possibilities for the future, positive and negative, and each just as potent and probable as the other. The entire country was poised on a knife-edge. In less than two years, the streets of downtown Benghazi, around the hotel where I lay staring into the ceiling, would become a battleground. The buildings, now occupied with families and their secrets, would stand as ghostly skeletons, charred and empty. Several of the people I met – I can count three from the event in the library alone – would be assassinated. We didn't know it then, but this was a precious window when justice, democracy and the rule of law were within reach. Soon, in the absence of a strong army and police force, armed groups would rule the day, seeking only to advance their power. Political factions would become entrenched, and, amidst the squabble, foreign militias and governments would violently enter, seeking their opportunity. The dead would mount. Universities and schools would close. Hospitals would become only partially operative. The situation would get so grim that the unimaginable would happen: people would come to long for the days of Qaddafi. It was of course impossible to imagine such a nightmare back in March 2012, yet in those night hours, lying there listening to the city in the dark, I could sense the possibility of horror.

Unable to sleep, I read the second of Father's two short stories in the anthology, entitled 'A Struggle with Fate'. It had an enigmatic beginning:

> I used to know him. It all seems so long ago and yet as though it had all happened yesterday. It was when his family still lived in our village. His father ran the café on the main road. The old mud bricks of the interior resembled skulls, each stamped with a sarcastic smile. I was one of the regulars who frequented the café. I would walk in and take any one of the wooden chairs scattered in a disorderly way around the place.

The unnamed narrator and the man referred to, the unspecified time, the ghostly bricks, the furniture set in no particular formation – all served to exacerbate my disorientation. The story told of the terrible misfortunes of a boy. We never learn his name and this, paradoxically, made him seem more intimate to me. Perhaps he was a fictional vessel into which the eighteen-year-old author could deposit his worst fears. The boy's 'struggle with fate' causes him to lose everything – his family, his home

– until he is left destitute. 'I wandered aimlessly, and did not find anywhere that would take me except that one place that had absorbed thousands of miserable souls before me: the street.' But then suddenly, gripped by fear and humiliation, he returns to the place where his father is buried in order to be able to 'shed the same tears once more'. After doing so, he goes out into the world and the story ends with him declaring, 'I decided to work and survive.'

That final sentence caught me. The boy's words matched an old mysterious instruction that, in the darkest moments and over the past quarter of a century since I lost my father, would come for me, sounding with the hard force of a warning bell, urgently ringing, *Work and survive, work and survive.* I heard it at university. I heard it when I worked as a stonemason after graduating. I heard it when I became a draughtsman and then an architectural designer. I heard it when, having devoted myself to writing, I worked in construction, painted houses and did odd jobs in a small market town in Bedfordshire. I heard it in the doubt of those days. I heard it when I stood at the edge of the Pont d'Arcole, a bridge in Paris, staring into the water. And I hear it still today. It never left me and yet it has never felt entirely my own. It belongs to some other presence implanted in me, one that knows better than anyone, perhaps even better than myself, that I am far closer to the precipice than I could conceive.

Running into that familiar call, which has for long represented my rescue, and finding it in the shape of the closing sentence of one of only two short stories my father ever published, was oddly consoling and disquieting. It flipped time on its head. The words were not coming to me from a parental authority now but through the eighteen-year-old who was yet to become my father, a man young enough to be my son, a talented and ambitious student who might have sought out my thoughts about becoming a writer. I reread the stories several times and, although I tried not to indulge the fantasy, I kept seeing myself complimenting him on his abilities and instincts, suggesting how he could improve his short stories, perhaps ending with a recommendation of what to read and taking down his address so as to send him books, perhaps buying him a subscription to some of the better literary journals, and then, on parting, it would be me now speaking the bell call to him, *Work and survive.*

The stories were a profound discovery. They were a gift sent back through time, opening a window on to the interior landscape of the young man who was to become my father. They were forward-looking, interested in finding a contemporary mode in which to write about Libya, but they were also engaged with the past. Their young protagonists were subject to the consequences of colonialism and its aftermath: the violence and poverty brought on by the Italian invasion. I stood at the window of my hotel room, watching the corniche stretch on both sides, the lamp-posts doing their best to illuminate it, and the sea unfolding, drawing itself out into the blackness. It was impossible not to read in the stories a latent expression of Father's anxiety. He had come close to losing his father. The extraordinary risks Grandfather Hamed had taken in confronting the Italian occupation, the many near-death experiences he had endured, which were colourfully chronicled in stories that have become part of the mythology of our family, must have represented for the young author a formative acquaintanceship with injustice. But I also imagine, from reading these narratives in which old men are vulnerable, that they made vivid to the teenager the universal fact that each one of us had, on too many occasions, come dangerously close to never having been born. In other words, he was a writer responding to ghosts and to history. Then, at some point, a crack opened and politics seeped in. I remember the great binges when, in between the relentless travel and political meetings, Father would bring me with him to the bookshop on Talaat Harb Square, in downtown Cairo. The bookseller knew him and would lead us up to the private flat upstairs, where all the banned books were kept. We would walk out with several black plastic bags full of novels the Egyptian censor had, for one reason or another, found objectionable. For the next two or three days Father would hardly emerge from his bedroom, reading one book after the next.

*

Grandfather Hamed lived an exceptionally long life. There are different estimates about his age when he died. Most agree that he was somewhere between 103 and 109 years old, although I was once emphatically told that he lived to 112. This would mean he was born somewhere between 1876 and 1885.

The *Royal Relief Atlas*, 'of all Parts of the World', published in London in October 1880, celebrates in its preface the 'great advance' that 'the scientific teaching of Geography' has made in recent years. It trumpets the Swiss pedagogue Johann Pestalozzi's maxim: 'Through the eye to the mind'. According to this, Libya was not even in the mind then. 'The countries into which [North] Africa is divided,' the *Atlas* tells us, 'are Morocco, governed by a Sultan, *cap.* Morocco; Algeria, a French colony, *cap.* Algiers; Tunis, governed by a Bey, *cap.* Tunis; Tripoli, governed by a Pasha, *cap.* Tripoli; Egypt, governed by a Khedive, *cap.* Cairo.' Then, to clarify, the authors inform us that 'All these, except Algiers, are tributaries of the Ottoman or Turkish Empire.' The closest we get to a mention of Libya is in the arching letters, stretching from Fezzan all the way to the Nile Delta, that read LIBYAN DESERT.

The first census carried out in Libya was in 1931. The population then was 700,000. Therefore, judging by how the population climbed after 1931, it would be reasonable to assume that back in the 1880s the population of the territory we now know as Libya was somewhere between 250,000 and 500,000. When Grandfather Hamed was born, Tripoli was a state, but the rest of the country was a vast and nearly empty landscape, with villages and towns dotted here and there, serving the trade and travel routes that ran up north from the continent and those that went east towards Mecca. Blo'thaah, Grandfather Hamed's ancestral home, hovered almost exactly mid-distance between Tripoli and Alexandria, with a three-week ride to either.

He was an only child, born in Ottoman Libya. He witnessed the Italian invasion, the reign of King Idris, and saw the two decades that followed Qaddafi's coup d'état of 1969. He was in his late forties or early fifties when my father was born, and near seventy on the birth of his youngest, Uncle Mahmoud. In a time where life expectancy for a Libyan man hovered somewhere around sixty-five, people thought him irresponsible. 'You won't live to see him walk,' they had told him. He saw Uncle Mahmoud graduate from university, marry and have children of his own. He died in his home in Ajdabiya in 1989.

Grandfather Hamed's house suited him. Ajdabiya then was a cluster of buildings in a vast emptiness. He never travelled in those days except the thirty or so kilometres to Blo'thaah, where he still preferred to spend the spring months, exposed further to what he called 'the expanse'.

'He felt free out there,' I remember my father once telling me. 'And, as a man who valued silence, it suited him perfectly.'

But even back in the days when Grandfather Hamed did travel to visit relatives, he was well known for going to great lengths not to spend a night at anyone's home. Perhaps that is where my unease at being a house-guest comes from. But once when I was a young boy, and after much insistence, my parents convinced him to pay us a visit in Tripoli. Finally he was going to see where we lived. I never saw my father more nervous or excited. Preparations intensified. Grandfather arrived in high spirits. He and my mother had a special fondness for one another. Grandfather seemed happy to have made the trip, but as the day wore on he became completely silent. My poor father and mother could not think what had caused the sudden change. The following day he packed his bag and wanted to leave. We all got in the car and began the long drive to Ajdabiya. My father drove, his father in the passenger seat beside him, and my mother, Ziad and I all crammed into the back. Grandfather's silence was particularly unsettling. He seemed to be holding his breath. He sat upright, his back not touching the backrest. As we left the capital and the wide desert plains opened all around us, he sighed and leant back.

'Finally,' he said, 'the horizon.'

My parents laughed and Grandfather told stories the whole way.

Grandfather's house stood in the centre of town. To my child's mind, it was the point from which not only Ajdabiya but the entire map of the world developed. Its architecture fostered this idea. For a young boy it was as mysterious and magical as a maze. And I cannot separate its various surprising turns, its seeming endlessness, its modest and somewhat austere aesthetic, from my grandfather's life and character. I often lost my way in its endless rooms, corridors and courtyards. Some windows looked out on to the street, some on to one of the courtyards, yet others, strangely, looked into other rooms. It was never quite clear whether you were indoors or outdoors. Some of its halls and corridors were roofless or had an opening through which a shaft of light leant in and turned with the hours. Some of its staircases took you outside, under the open sky, before winding back in. The décor was plain.

The walls were plastered and painted in two halves: the lower part dark, usually in a strong blue or green or purple, and the upper in white or pale pink or pastel yellow. Some floors were tiled and others were covered unevenly – like cream cheese on toast, I used to think – in a material similar to concrete. Where there was heavy traffic, such as the entrance, it shone dark and smooth. Bare bulbs hung from the ceilings and there was hardly any furniture. The house was like one of my grandfather's long poems: austere, unpredictable, plain, unfinished, yet inhabited. Ever since I can remember, I have found the unfinished state of much of modern Libya's architecture unsettling. It expresses neglect more actively than, say, ruins or old decaying structures. When something is built, we assume it to have been built out of a sense of necessity, intent or desire. Therefore, we associate its incompleteness with deliberate negligence and carelessness, or else sudden impotence. These half-finished buildings seem more of an affront, more offensive and indeed oppressive, than a finished building that has fallen on hard times. The epidemic is on such a scale – exterior walls left without render, unpainted – that it is hard not to read it as a lack of self-regard. Our unfinished homes are, in other words, a reflection of our present. Just as we have made them, they have come to define us. But perhaps I am wrong, allowing my taste, my liking for the meticulous and finished surface, to get in the way. Because I know Grandfather Hamed found great freedom in his house and in his poems. To him – in architecture, in literature, as in good manners – grandeur, good taste and such were best expressed through a modest minimalism that shied away from the polished surface. He didn't like things that glittered. He never praised himself, not even obliquely.

Grandfather Hamed would lie down in the far corner of the hall, which was a large rectangular room lined with cushions. One of the photographs I keep of him – a copy of which I sent to the Canadian forensic artist to help her produce a likeness of how Father might look today – shows Grandfather Hamed lying in that same corner. His exceptionally tall, lean figure is spread across the cushions, the radio and a couple of cartons of Kent cigarettes beside him. His face looks back at me with gentle solemnity. A cigarette is between his long and dark fingers, the thin line of smoke rising above his head.

The impression I have always had of being from a horizontal family probably originated in these early encounters with my grandfather. It is in part literal, to do with our tendency, whenever reading or conversing casually or needing to carefully consider a particular problem, to reach for the nearest pillow. But also the ways in which we affect and come at one another have always had a sideways motion. The image that comes to mind is that of spilt milk, spreading as it spends itself. Perhaps this is why in our gatherings there has always been, besides the exuberance and warmth, that unspoken desperation to gather up the pieces.

I remember him beckoning me over once, gathering his fingers round a troublesome button on my shirt and feeding it through its hole, straightening my collar, and then running a trembling hand over my hair with a strange, feathery touch, as though he were barely there. I asked him about fighting the Italians. I don't remember what he said, if indeed he said anything at all about it. Another time, someone, perhaps it was Uncle Mahmoud, retold the story – a little louder than necessary, because Grandfather Hamed was hard of hearing by then – of the time when Grandfather was shot in battle. He was brought to a house in a nearby village. No one could stop the bleeding. A young girl known for her intelligence ran to the sorceress in the neighbouring town. The old woman gave her a small pouch of white powder and told the girl to place it on the wound. The bleeding stopped and a few days later Grandfather Hamed was well enough to rejoin the resistance. I had heard the story before but never in the presence of its protagonist. Seeing how relentlessly I was staring at him, my grandfather patted the seat beside him.

'You needn't look so sad,' he said.

'Where did they shoot you?' I asked.

He paused for a moment and then unbuttoned his shirt. He pulled the fabric over his shoulder and showed me where the bullet had entered: a small rosette just beneath the collarbone.

'Show me where it came out,' I said, and pulled his shirt further down to see his back, expecting to find an identical scar. Instead, the skin there was completely smooth.

'Where is it?' I asked.

'Still inside,' he said.

I remember how terribly upset I became, not immediately but a little while later, when I returned to ask if there was no way of removing it. To distract me, he took me on a walk. People stopped and greeted him. He introduced me. 'I would like you to meet my grandson Hisham. He has come all the way from Tripoli especially to see me.'

*

I had been lucky, it was communicated to me in countless wordless ways, to be Hamed Matar's grandson. When I was a child I could see that many people around me idealized him, and, because that kind of idealizing serves more to obscure than reveal a man, it clouded my early impressions of him and made me even more curious about what kind of man he was. I paid close attention whenever his name was mentioned. I knew that his life had been deeply disrupted by the Italian invasion, and, because of the scarcity of accounts from that period, the gaps in Grandfather Hamed's life are in part connected to the wider story of the occupation. The trend of silence continued. Even today, to be Libyan is to live with questions.

All the books on the modern history of the country could fit neatly on a couple of shelves. The best amongst them is slim enough to slide into my coat pocket and be read in a day or two. There are many other histories, of course, concerning those who, over the past three millennia, occupied Libya: the Phoenicians, the Greeks, the Romans, the Ottomans and, most recently, the Italians. A Libyan hoping to glimpse something of that past must, like an intruder at a private party, enter such books in the full knowledge that most of them were not written by or for him, and, therefore, at heart, they are accounts concerning the lives of others, their adventures and misadventures in Libya, as though one's country is but an opportunity for foreigners to exorcize their demons and live out their ambitions.

This shortage of historical accounts is partly a result of the painful birth of modern Libya. The country experienced one of the most violent campaigns in the history of colonial repression. The Italians arrived in 1911. They had calculated rightly that the few Ottoman garrisons based in coastal towns would quickly fall. What they did not expect, however, was the determination, discipline and stamina of local resistance. Between 1911 and 1916 – and in retaliation for a popular uprising in Tripoli, what the Italians term the 'Arab Revolt' – more than 5,000 men were banished from the city and sent to small islands scattered around Italy – islands such as Isole Tremiti, Ponza, Ustica and Favignana – and kept in prisons there. Five thousand is a large number, but it is even more significant given that the population of Tripoli at that time was only 30,000. In other words, one in every six inhabitants of the Libyan capital was kidnapped and made to disappear. The damage was more lasting because the Italian authorities selected the most noted and distinguished men: scholars, jurists, wealthy traders and bureaucrats. The conditions aboard ship were so bad that during the journey, which couldn't have taken much more than a couple of days, hundreds of prisoners died. Some historians claim that one-quarter of the 5,000 men lost their lives during the passage. The majority of those who reached the island prisons perished in captivity. There appears to be no record of survivors from those prisoners. It is an extraordinary example of a European occupying power devastating a city. Yet, as with Italian crimes in Libya in general, it is an event little known today. It has been clouded over by the greater horrors inflicted by the Italians later, which are, alas, only slightly less obscure.

Almost immediately after the Italians arrived, a local leader emerged. Omar al-Mukhtar, the man we grew up referring to affectionately as Sidi Omar, was part of the Senussi order, a mystical religious family that ran schools and charities from Cyrenaica in the north-east of the country all the way west into Algeria and further south into sub-Saharan Africa. Its patriarch, Idris, was to become king and Libya's first head of state after independence. Despite having very few resources, Omar al-Mukhtar led Libya's tribesmen on horseback in what became a very effective campaign. But after the Fascists marched on Rome in 1922 and Benito Mussolini seized power, the destruction and slaughter took on a massive scale. Airpower was employed to gas and bomb villages. The policy was that of depopulation. History remembers Mussolini as the buffoonish Fascist, the ineffective silly man of Italy who led a lame military campaign in the Second World War, but in Libya he oversaw a campaign of genocide.

The tribal population was marched on foot to several concentration camps across the country. Every family lost members in these camps. Several of my forebears died there. Stories of torture, humiliation and famine have filtered down through the generations. The Danish journalist Knud Holmboe, who was travelling through Libya at the time, is the only Western reporter I know of to have visited the camps. His book *Desert Encounter: An Adventurous Journey through Italian Africa* is a deeply troubling account and a rare document. His Italian host, an army officer, brings him to one of the camps:

> The camp was immense. It contained at least fifteen hundred tents and had a population of six to eight thousand people. It was fenced in with barbed wire, and there were guards with machine-guns at every entrance. As we drove up among the tents children came running towards us. They were in rags and hungry, half-starved, but evidently they were accustomed to getting money from the Commandant on his visits, for they stretched out their hands and shouted in Italian: *'Un soldo, signore, un soldo!'* ... The Bedouins gathered round us. They looked incredibly ragged. On their feet were hides tied with string; their burnouses were a patchwork of all kinds of multi-coloured pieces. Many of them seemed ill and wretched, limping along with crooked backs, or with arms and legs that were terribly deformed.

Holmboe is outraged, but he tries to keep his opinions to himself lest he lose the access his Italian hosts have granted him. But in a moment in the camp, when no one can hear, he speaks to an internee in his perfect Arabic:

> I asked one of the Bedouins:
> 'Where is Ahmar Moktar [Omar al-Mukhtar]?'

The Bedouin showed his white teeth in a smile.

'Ahmar Moktar,' he said, making a sweeping gesture towards the mountains with his arms, 'is everywhere in the mountains and the valleys.'

The book infuriated the Italians. They banned it and arrested its author. A few months after Holmboe's release the Dane was found south of Aqaba, in Jordan, murdered. Suspicions that Italian intelligence assassinated him remain.

It is not clear how many perished in the camps. Official Italian census records show that the population of Cyrenaica plummeted from 225,000 to 142,000. The orphans, numbering in the thousands, were sent to Fascist camps to be 're-educated'. Brand-new planes machine-gunned herds of livestock. An Italian general boasted that between 1930 and 1931 the army reduced the number of sheep and goats from 270,000 to 67,000. As a consequence, many people starved to death.

The Libyan poet Rajab Abuhweish, who was a scholar and a teacher and later served as a jurist in Algeria and Chad, returned home to Libya in 1911 to join the resistance. When the Italians attacked his village, they burnt down the houses and poured concrete in the well. They marched him and his family, along with the rest of the villagers, 400 kilometres to the infamous El-Agheila concentration camp. Being forbidden pens and paper, he composed a thirty-stanza-long poem that he committed to memory. It was memorized by others and that way spread across the country. It so fortified the spirit of resistance that when the Italians uncovered the identity of its author they whipped him. The poem is called 'I Have No Illness But'. It opens:

> I have no illness but El-Agheila camp,
> the imprisonment of the tribe
> and being cut off from the open country.

> I have no illness but this endless despair,
> the scarcity of things and the loss of my red mare,
> its forelegs black to the hoofs.

> When disaster struck
> she galloped, stretching her long neck
> with incomparable beauty.

Rajab Abuhweish's poem was one of the first I ever encountered. It was taught at school as part of the story of Libya's struggle for independence. It had such an impact on me. The twenty-third stanza in particular, and its image of the aged child, haunted me when I was a boy:

> I have no illness but the loss of noble folk
> and the foul ones who now,
> with calamitous, shameless faces, govern us.

> How many a child have they taken and whipped?
> The poor young flowers return confused,
> made old without having lived.

After independence, Rajab Abuhweish returned to teaching and served as an adviser to King Idris's senate. He died in 1952.

*

Grandfather Hamed had also joined the resistance in the east of the country, under the leadership of Omar al-Mukhtar, immediately after the 1911 invasion. But then eight years later, in 1919, he suddenly and in great haste took his young family and escaped to Alexandria. This puzzled me, because Libyans who fought under Omar al-Mukhtar and who, like Grandfather Hamed, had some private means – in his case, land – to fund their move did not begin to emigrate to Egypt for another twelve years. To be precise, it wasn't until the 11th of September 1931 that the resistance received its mortal blow. Omar al-Mukhtar, who was by then seventy-three years old, was wounded in a rapid retreat and fell off his horse. Five days later, and after a show trial, the great man was hanged on the outskirts of Benghazi. Just as the Qaddafi regime did half a century later, when traffic was diverted so that commuters were obliged to witness the bodies of the students dangling in the garden of the Benghazi cathedral, the Italian colonial administration made sure that Sidi Omar's execution was attended by as large a number of Libyans as possible. It broke the spirit of the country. Over the next two years the resistance, a formidable force that had inspired several independence movements around the world, disintegrated. It was then that many of its members fled to Alexandria. A generation later, my father, having observed how Qaddafi's dictatorship had decimated the opposition, also emigrated to neighbouring Egypt in the hope of rebuilding dissent from abroad. But what on earth drove Grandfather Hamed to leave in a hurry in 1919, when the Libyan tribesmen on horseback, armed with old Ottoman rifles and what they could capture from the enemy, seemed close to defeating a European power?

One explanation – told in different versions, depending on who is telling the story – is that one night, shortly before Grandfather Hamed fled to Alexandria, he hid behind a street corner in downtown Benghazi. A high-ranking Italian officer had popped out in the late hours for a stroll and to catch the bakery before it closed. He walked home clutching the sack of bread in one hand and nibbling an end of a baguette with the other. Grandfather Hamed pulled the officer into the shadows and stabbed him in the neck. A few days later he was in Alexandria.

I find it difficult to believe the attack was random, responding to an opportunity to hurt the enemy or provoked by hunger. In the resistance, Grandfather Hamed was known for being a good shot, an excellent rider and an effective strategist who rarely took unnecessary risks. The war was fought in battles away from heavily populated centres. Omar al-Mukhtar's men were determined not to descend to the tactics of the enemy and target women, children or the civilian population. They did not operate in towns and cities. When they ambushed, they ambushed military columns and garrisons, not an officer walking home from the bakery. This increases the credibility of some of the other accounts of the story, which claim that Grandfather Hamed did not kill the Italian for bread but rather to settle a score with that particular man, whom he had been stalking for days. Perhaps, like the family in Father's story 'In the Stillness of the Night', Grandfather Hamed's family and livestock had been attacked by Italian troops and perhaps it had not ended as well for them as it had for Ahmed, his uncle and cousin Aisha. I suspect others knew of the enmity and therefore might have been able to deduce who killed the Italian, which would explain why Grandfather Hamed felt it necessary to quickly leave Libya, the country he nearly died defending, and take his family with him.

But, of course, this whole story may not be true. He may not have killed the officer, and moved simply because he had had enough of the war and wanted to bring up his young family in peace and in the cultured city of great opportunities that Alexandria was in those days. Whatever the reason, he settled in Alexandria and remained there for the next twenty years. Having shown no particular interest in business up until then, he became a successful tradesman and owned a large house in one of the best neighbourhoods. It was said that when the rings around the eyelets of his handmade leather boots wore away, he had them replaced in platinum in the hope that he would not have to return to the cobbler. But then at the height of his success in the early 1930s, after the execution of Sidi Omar, when the noose was tightening, Grandfather Hamed, like his son many years later, was arrested in Egypt. He was handed over to the Italian authorities and sent to Italy. The record is not clear whether he went to Bologna or Padua. Whenever the colonial authorities took a member of the Libyan resistance to Italy, it meant only one thing: execution. And the bodies of the deceased were never returned to the families. The day after my grandfather was taken, droves of people came to the house to offer their condolences. My grandmother put on her black clothes, rented a couple of hundred chairs and hired a graduate from Al-Azhar University, who, over the next three days, sat cross-legged in the main hall and recited the entire Quran.

What no one knew was that a few days into his captivity, Grandfather Hamed escaped, made his way to the nearest port and persuaded a fisherman to take him to a ship that had just set off for Alexandria. The fisherman's boat edged close to the rear steps. Grandfather Hamed climbed in unnoticed. He hid in the engine room. When night fell, he rummaged in the bins for leftovers. A few days later, the ship docked in Alexandria. Several weeks after Grandfather Hamed's capture and after all the mourners had returned to their homes, my grandmother was woken up in the middle of the night by heavy knocking at the door. She was frightened, but when she opened the door she nearly fainted. She kept squeezing her husband's hand to make sure he was not a ghost. He closed his business and in a few days the family was back in Libya. I found the story puzzling. Why did he return so quickly and place himself in even more danger?

I recently contacted the historian Nicola Labanca, an authority on the Italian colonial period in Libya. I was hoping he could direct me to an archive where I might find a record of Grandfather's arrest. Labanca said there was no such archive, that the Italians then kept few records, most of which were destroyed during the war. I was back in that familiar place, a place of shadows where the only way to engage with what happened is through the imagination, an activity that serves only to excite the past, multiplying its possibilities, like a house with endless rooms, inescapable and haunted. According to Labanca, who kindly indulged my questions, it would have been highly unlikely that my grandfather was taken to Italy for trial. 'The Libyans,' he said, 'who were brought to Italy were brought here for two things and two things only: to be tortured for information and then killed. There was no trial for Libyans.' On the other hand, the timing of his return to Libya made sense. In the years after the execution of Omar al-Mukhtar, Mussolini was very keen on bringing wealthy Libyans living abroad back to Libya. He wanted to do this for two reasons: to help the economy, particularly that of Cyrenaica, which had suffered most during the later years of the fighting; and to have such dangerous men, who were probably pouring money into efforts to re-establish the resistance, back in the country, where they could be monitored. This, Labanca said, would better explain why my grandfather returned. 'He couldn't have escaped,' Labanca said. 'He was probably confronted with the two stark choices the Italian authorities gave wealthy Libyans living in exile: die or return to Libya.'

*

When my grandmother passed away, Father, in Cairo and unable to attend the funeral, grew quiet. For several days he became terribly distant, as though grief were a far-away country. When several years later Grandfather Hamed died, my father fell into an even deeper despair, although Grandfather had been extremely old and it was expected.

It was late in 1989. Ziad and I were at university in London, and our parents were visiting. Mother, with her usual anxiety about breaking bad news, told me in the morning, after I had caught her crying, that Grandfather Hamed was unwell.

'He might not make it,' she said.

I headed to class but turned back when I remembered how, when I was seven, my mother came to find me in our garden at the back of our house in Tripoli and said the same thing about her father. He would die later that day.

Ziad, Mother and I waited for Father to return from his morning errands. Mother sat him down and tried, as gently as she could, to hand him the bad news. She and Ziad were visibly moved, but I remember only being terrified. Without saying a word, Father stood up and went to his room. We followed him. He sat on the edge of the bed and covered his face. I had never seen him cry before. He kept his palms pressed tightly to his face. I could hear a low howl, as though he were screaming from a long way away.

A few months later my father disappeared.

Those two events – the death of Grandfather Hamed and Father falling into the abyss of Qaddafi's dungeons –

are connected in my mind also because, in the days that followed my grandfather's death, a new desperation took hold of my father. I recall thinking, whenever I would catch him sitting alone, there is a terribly impatient man. I detected it too in the occasional photograph Mother included with her letters, showing him alone or the two of them standing side by side. I found this new idea of his impatience peculiar. My father had always been the very expression of patience. Whenever I showed frustration, he would say that word, 'Patience', as though it were a vow, and then add the nickname he had fashioned for me, 'Sharh el-Bal', 'The Soother of Mind'; the name was no doubt intended to help me cure myself of my own impatience. He would often quote the twice-repeated line from the chapter 'Soothing' in the Quran: 'With hardship comes ease. With hardship comes ease.' But the death of Grandfather Hamed disturbed him, and disturbed him, as it turned out, irrevocably. He lost his way. He became less careful.

Three years after his abduction – three years of utter silence – an audio-cassette letter reached us, with his voice recorded over a recital of the Quran that the prisoners had been given. After forty minutes of poised speech, after he had said goodbye and therefore could have pressed the 'stop' button, I heard it come as though from within me, that same soft howl again, this time from an even deeper well. For a reason I will never know, he chose not to erase it. He wanted us to hear it.

*

Shortly before he disappeared, my father had confided in me a secret. In the years following my grandmother's death, Father, on more than one occasion, would dress as an Egyptian farmer and, bearing a fake passport, slip through the Egyptian–Libyan border. He would make his way to Ajdabiya to see his father.

'Brief nocturnal visits that rarely lasted more than an hour or two,' Father told me.

We were both lying on my narrow bed in London, facing each other. Out of respect, I had my feet bent away from him, but his were right beside me, so I could press my thumbs into the soles with the strength I knew he liked.

'Was he surprised to see you?' I asked.

'No, somehow he always expected it,' my father said.

They would sit in the corner of Grandfather's large room, whispering in the dark, before Father would kiss his father's hand and forehead and begin the dangerous long journey back.

'You didn't see your brothers and sisters?' I asked.

'Too dangerous,' he said.

My father too had a father who knew how to keep a secret.

All in all, Father told me, he had done this 'about' three times.

'Reckless,' I said.

'Now that he's gone,' he said to reassure me, 'there's no need to worry.'

And now, after a quarter of a century of not seeing my father, I would take the same risks to see him, even if for only an hour or two.

I have wondered ever since about the timing, about why my father chose that particular moment to tell me of his secret visits to Ajdabiya. I had then assumed it was because Grandfather Hamed had just passed away, but now I am not sure. On that same tape, which over the past twenty-five years I have managed to listen to only five times, he says, 'Don't come looking for me,' and every time that line brings to mind that afternoon when he and I were stretched, side by side, facing one another, on my narrow bed in London. His words 'Now that he's gone, there's no need to worry,' which I had then taken as reassurance, I have come to see as a warning that I had missed. What he really meant was, now that his father was gone, he could take even greater risks.

15. Maximilian

Not knowing when my father ceased to exist has further complicated the boundary between life and death. But this can only partly explain why for the longest time, even before my father's disappearance, the commonplace occurrence of being able to point to a calendar and say, it was on that exact day that a particular person's life ended, has always seemed inaccurate. Perhaps we should be with the bereaved, cover our ears and insist, 'No, he is not dead.' Perhaps that is not only a denial of terrible news but also a momentary recognition of a truth, one that passes and is buried along with the deceased. Disbelief is the right instinct, for how can the dead really be dead? I think this because absence has never seemed empty or passive but rather a busy place, vocal and insistent. As Aristotle writes, 'The theory that the void exists involves the existence of place: for one would define void as place bereft of body.' He says nothing of time here, and time is surely part of it all, of how we try to accommodate the absence. Perhaps this is why, in countless cultures, people in mourning rock or sway from side to side – not only to recall infancy and the mother's heartbeat, but to keep time. Only time can hope to fill the void. The body of my father is gone, but his place is here and occupied by something that cannot just be called memory. It is alive and current. How could the complexities of being, the mechanics of our anatomy, the intelligence of our biology, and the endless firmament of our interiority – the thoughts and questions and yearnings and hopes and hunger and desire and the thousand and one contradictions that inhabit us at any given moment – ever have an ending that could be marked by a date on a calendar? Hasn't it always seemed that way? Haven't I always detected the confusion of funerals, the uncertainty of cemeteries, the bewilderment of a headstone? Perhaps memorials and all the sacred and secular rituals of mourning across our human history are but failed gestures. The dead live with us. Grief is not a whodunnit story, or a puzzle to solve, but an active and vibrant enterprise. It is hard, honest work. It can break your back. It is part of one's initiation into death and – I don't know why, I have no way of justifying it – it is a hopeful part at that. What is extraordinary is that, given everything that has happened, the natural alignment of the heart remains towards the light. It is in that direction that there is the least resistance. I have never understood this. Not intellectually anyway. But it is somehow in the body, in the physical knowledge of the eternity of each moment, in the expansive nature of time and space, that declarative statements such as 'He is dead' are not precise. My father is both dead and alive. I do not have a grammar for him. He is in the past, present and future. Even if I had held his hand, and felt it slacken, as he exhaled his last breath, I would still, I believe, every time I refer to him, pause to search for the right tense. I suspect many men who have buried their fathers feel the same. I am no different. I live, as we all live, in the aftermath.

A few days after my return to Libya, I flew to Rome and stood in front of Titian's *The Martyrdom of Saint Lawrence*. I had gone to Rome specially to see the exhibition. Several of the Italian artist's masterpieces were collected in one place. Most of them had never been in the same room before. I had seen *The Martyrdom of Saint Lawrence* in countless reproductions – in books and postcards and once in a large poster on a friend's wall – but none prepared me for the real thing. It is massive in scale, measuring just less than five metres high by three metres wide. It is impossible to ignore Lawrence's suffering. I stood there till closing time. I watched the fit body of a man, a body still good, pinned to a wooden bench. I thought of the carpenter who had constructed the bench. I saw the daughter handing him a glass of water. The bench had been constructed carefully to play its part effectively: to hold up the body until, at the right moment, it would burn too and crumble. But we are at an earlier stage. The bench is still holding up well. The fire beneath it is being stoked by a half-naked figure. Like the carpenter – or perhaps he is the carpenter – the man is diligent in his work. There is no end to Lawrence's torment. He is surrounded by efficient men. Behind him stands one with strong arms. He is working hard to keep the victim down. Agony is twisting Lawrence's body. His head is thrown back. The brute, either out of strain or shame, looks away. Meanwhile another man, barefaced, is stabbing Lawrence in the ribs, poking him as he might a chained animal, safe in the knowledge it cannot reach him. The light comes from the fires: the one burning beneath Lawrence and those of the torches of bystanders watching the spectacle. The only other source of light is a gash in the heavens, its edges bubbling with clouds, as though the sky has developed an infected wound. The moon's glow pours through. It touches Lawrence's outstretched hand and lights up his fingertips. There is a strange detail: Lawrence's left foot is caught in a peculiar position, dangling off the bench, floating in the flames, as if enjoying the fire.

I find certain paintings mysterious. I am drawn to them as I am to certain individuals. I have been interested in art, architecture and music for as long as I can remember, but the fascination with pictures changed when I was nineteen, the year I lost my father. The usual way of going to a gallery, of spending a couple of hours passing from one painting to the next, until one finally comes to the end, no longer worked. In fact, it overwhelmed me. More than once I thought of screaming. Yet I kept returning, of my own volition. That was when I began what was meant to be a temporary solution to the problem but that has, over the years, become an integral part of my life. I was living near the National Gallery, and entry was free, so I thought I would choose one painting and pay it a brief, fifteen-minute visit every day and do this five times a week. I would switch to another painting whenever I felt I had exhausted my interest. In those days, that usually took a week; now, partly because I am able to visit the museum only once or twice a week, it can take much longer, sometimes as long as a year, before I move on to a new painting.

For the past twenty-five years I have kept up this vigil in all the places I have lived. That day in Rome, after I had seen my country for the first time in thirty-three years, after I had found out all I could find out about what had befallen my father, I sat on the floor of the emptying gallery, looking up at *The Martyrdom of Saint Lawrence*, sketching in my notebook – in part to help me look, but in greater part to justify the length of time I was spending in front of the picture. And then, without noticing that I had surrendered to them, I was surrounded by sounds and images, coming at me in sharp broken fragments, of Father's final moments: what they might have told him, what his last words might have been, the past and how it seemed to him then.

*

As with the carpenter of Lawrence's bench, the architect of Abu Salim had applied practical thought to the design of Father's prison cell, the room Father had ironically referred to in his letter as the 'noble palace'. One of the things humanity seems to agree upon is how prisons should look and function. The design of Abu Salim adheres to this universal code. The man who designed the cell had never stood in it; in fact, he had never seen his building in the flesh. He had sat at a drawing table in another country and, between meals, visits to the bathroom and other obligations, he considered standard measurements, capacity, materials and layout. He opted for prefabricated concrete walls, which were then loaded on to ships and transported to Tripoli. The foreign labourers who assembled the building were allotted reasonable working hours. Lunches were provided. Construction happened in record time. Locals living near the building site commented on how one day it wasn't there and the next day there it was. The architect had specified that the manufacturer puncture a round hole at the dead centre of each prefabricated wall. This way, when the crane lifted the ready made slab, it rose in perfect balance, as straight as a guillotine. The holes were then plastered over and concealed. But later, when the cells filled up, prisoners discovered their location. They found out that if they chipped away at the plaster, they could open a channel to the next cell, one big enough to pass a book through. I know this because Father describes these holes in his letter, then writes, 'All sorts of goods pass this way. None are more precious than books.' And then he adds, 'The prison is a great library,' which I found hard to believe. Every February, returning from the Cairo Book Fair, we would struggle to fit all the books my father bought in the boot and often had to hire a taxi. Every time I dared to read Father's prison letters, my mind would search for signs of how he might have changed, been altered or reduced by his incarceration. Regardless of their quality, books passed through these openings, which were concealed by day and opened at night. They created a network connecting nearly all the cells. It was the unintended consequence of the architect's decision. The floor plan was made up of wards constructed at right angles, grouped around rectangular open spaces. These courtyards were the only places where prisoners could walk under the sky. It was in these that, on the 29th of June 1996, 1,270 prisoners were executed. Although I never believed it, it is possible that Father was amongst them.

A former prisoner I had met in 2004 told me that in April 1996, two months before the massacre, Father was taken away from his cell. His few belongings were left behind and later sold by the guards to other prisoners. Father was then moved to another wing in the same prison, or to another prison, or executed straight away, or brought back two months later to die with the others, or killed later at an unknown time and place.

Over the past two and a half decades, I have followed up every scrap of information concerning life in Abu Salim. I read every account I could find, and, whenever I heard of a former inmate who had left the country, I tried to make contact and meet him. On one occasion, I flew all the way to Oklahoma. I always went to these meetings with the same mixture of dread and tired hope. There was modesty in these men, one that expressed itself in not wanting to disclose all the facts at once. It reminded me of the misplaced pride of those who, having had a great fortune bestowed upon them, try to make light of their privilege. I thought this critically, out of frustration, for I often had to restrain myself, limit my questions, which I tried to ask with the least possible urgency. I met so many people, so many names. I know so many names. There are times when I lie on my back and close my eyes and see them floating above me like moths.

In one such encounter, I met a man in an empty London café. We sat at a table in the back corner, from where the entire place could be seen. He sat with his back to the entrance, and I kept an eye on who came in. This was in the years after 2004, when Tony Blair had gone to Libya and stood shaking hands with Muammar Qaddafi. Ziad called me that afternoon. 'Now we have lost everything,' he said. The dictatorship became more powerful than ever before. Some of its worst criminals began to buy houses in London. Qaddafi's spymaster, Moussa Koussa – who, in 1980, had been expelled from Britain after advocating strong support, in an interview with *The Times*, for Libya's policy of assassinating opponents abroad – was now a regular visitor. Following Tony Blair's visit, the British capital became the number one place from which the Libyan secret service could monitor Libyans abroad. Britain helped to deliver dissidents to Tripoli. The Libyan Investment Authority, a corrupt institution that claimed to manage the national wealth, was based in London. The LIA purchased hotels, real estate and various investments, often in the names of individuals from the Qaddafi inner circle. Noted and powerful British financiers were board members. The dictator's son and heir apparent, Seif el-Islam Qaddafi, became the darling of the British establishment. The London School of Economics awarded him a PhD, which later turned out to be fraudulent. Several British academics, politicians, lawyers and public relations agencies began working hard at washing the blood off the Libyan regime. None of us felt safe. Officials from the Libyan embassy attended the first reading I gave from my first novel. A report was sent to Tripoli and I became a watched man. It was deemed no longer safe for me to visit my family in Egypt, which caused a second exile. When friends or relatives visited London, many did not feel it was prudent to be seen with me. Every time I gave an interview criticizing the dictatorship, I walked around for days feeling the weight of the regime on my back. It was under such circumstances that the former prisoner and I met in the café in London.

He told me that, although the prison authorities made sure Father did not mix with the other prisoners, he had managed to be in contact with my father.

'We exchanged messages through the passages.'

'So you never actually saw him?' I asked.

'Only from a distance,' he said, and explained how he used to stand on the shoulders of one of his cellmates and watch through the high windows as Father paced the courtyard alone.

I looked into the man's face as he told me this. I felt the powerful urge not so much to know how Father had appeared to him but literally to possess his eyes, the eyes with which he had seen my father, to pluck them out of the man's skull and insert them into mine.

On another occasion around that time, I spoke to a former inmate who had worked as a cook in the prison kitchen during the period when the massacre took place. After the shooting, which went on for several hours and was like 'a drill inside your head', the guards brought him a box full of blood-stained watches and rings. They asked him to wash them clean. Someone had obviously forgotten to ask the prisoners to take off their watches and wedding rings, or, more likely, the guards, who managed a clandestine economy of confiscated and stolen goods, could not be seen stealing in front of their superiors and, when no one was looking, went later from body to body, quickly unstrapping watches and pulling rings. The cook made a mental note of the number of watches. This is how his testimony, during those years when all news of the massacre was suppressed, gave campaigners and human rights organizations an early indication of the numbers killed that day.

*

Father warns in his first letter, which we received in 1993, that no one should learn of the correspondence he has sent: 'or else,' he writes, 'I will fall into a bottomless abyss. I would prefer to die under torture than give the names of those who have delivered this letter.'

Mother, Ziad and I were in my room in Cairo, crouched on the floor by the foot of my bed. I cannot remember why we came to be reading it in this odd position. It was as if the letter contained an explosive device we had hoped to render safe. This was not the first time we had read the letter but it was the first rereading, a day after the immediate shock of having received it and learning that Father was not in a secret location in Cairo, as the Egyptian authorities had led us to believe, but in Abu Salim prison in Tripoli. Mother started reading, then stopped. Ziad took over. Then it was my turn to continue. And so it went, until we reached the final line. On more than one occasion, Ziad and I had to ask Mother to help us make out a word. No one knows Father's handwriting better than she does.

Our gaze was so determined we could hardly see. Like figures moving in a fog. And each one of us worried about losing the others. But grief is a divider; it moved each one of us into a territory of private shadows, where the torment was incommunicable, so horribly outside of language.

I kept thinking about the word 'fall'. Why did he say 'fall into a bottomless abyss' when surely he meant 'be thrown'? 'Fall' implied he had a role in the matter. It brought to mind a man being taken to the edge of sanity, then falling. And the description of the abyss as bottomless unnerved me even further. The word 'abyss' was bad enough; why add the adjective? That, for reasons I could not explain then, upset me more than any other detail in the letter. It shook a place in me that remains dislodged. By choosing to define the kind of abyss he would have been cast into, Father had, unintentionally, revealed a dark truth. In this underworld from where Father was writing, there were clearly a variety of abysses. Furthermore, he had, by the time he wrote his letter, been acquainted with several of them. Some had seemed bottomless but then turned out not to be. But the threat the letter presented was one that would not offer any relief.

One of the frustrations of prison life, which is also one of its intended consequences, is that the prisoner is made ineffective. He is unable to be of much use. The aim is to render him powerless. The frustration builds up until he takes an unreasonable risk. In October 1995, five and a half years after his abduction, Father crossed this line. He wrote a letter to Saber Majid, a wealthy Libyan dissident living in London. In it, Father explained that a fellow-prisoner's family had fallen on hard times and that he was writing to ask for a loan of $8,000 to be given to the bearer of the letter. 'Let me be clear,' Father writes. 'This is a loan which I will repay you once I am free. If that day never comes, then my sons, Ziad and Hisham, will repay it.' Included in the letter is the usual warning, emphasizing the importance of keeping the letter secret. When Ziad and I offered to repay Father's loan, the man revealed that he had never given the bearer the money. This angered us. After all, Father and several others had risked their lives to deliver the message. Saber Majid simply said, 'I couldn't be sure the man who brought me the letter was genuine.' We asked if he knew how to reach the man. He said he didn't and couldn't even recall his name. Furthermore, whether deliberately or out of sheer stupidity, Saber Majid published Father's letter in an Arabic-language news-paper. The bottomless abyss opened up.

In 2011, when Tripoli fell and all the prisoners in Abu Salim were released, Ziad met a man who had been in the cell next door to Father's. The man recalled the interrogation provoked by the publication of the letter. He told Ziad he heard it by placing his ear against the opening in the wall. He relayed it in the following way:

'The interrogator said: "I want to know who delivered the letter."

'Your father responded: "What letter?"

'The interrogator said: "The letter in this newspaper. I want the name of the prisoner you gave it to and the one on the outside who delivered it."

'Your father said: "I will tell you. I wrote that letter with my own hand, I folded the piece of paper several times, and I gave it to you. If anyone asks me, I will tell them you delivered it."

'After this,' the prisoner told Ziad, 'Mr Jaballa was tortured so badly that he could not stand up at night to talk to us. It went on for three days. Then they moved him.'

*

I have always known who had delivered the letters to us. It was my cousin Nasser al-Tashani, Marwan and Nafa's older brother. I remember the day in Cairo when the doorbell rang and he walked in. He had not told us that he was coming all the way from Libya. We were surprised and pleased to see him. But, instead of greeting us, he went straight to the stereo system – as I remember it, a song by Oum Kalthum was playing – and he turned the volume all the way up. He then embraced Mother and whispered something in her ear. We all watched as he brought out a white piece of paper folded several times over so that it was the size of a postage stamp.

Over the years, Nasser never told me the name of the other man inside Abu Salim prison who had handed him the letters. All I knew was that the man was a friend whom Nasser visited from time to time. I have many times wondered if Father, when he was sent down into the bottomless abyss, yielded the man's name under torture. That the authorities never questioned Nasser boded well, but it could also have meant that the authorities, having extracted the name of the prisoner from my father, then failed to extract Nasser's name from the prisoner. I was ashamed to think these thoughts, for who could blame a man for speaking under torture, let alone one's own father? But it was not just pride. I somehow needed to know that he did not break, that he went on retaining what was his, that there was a place they could never reach.

One morning in Benghazi, the telephone in our hotel room rang. When I answered, a man's voice said, 'You don't know me, but your father was like a father to me. I'm downstairs. Would love to meet you.'

When the lift doors opened, I found the man standing in the lobby. He was perhaps five years older than me. He had an exceptionally healthy-looking face. I remember thinking this at the time. Clear eyes and clear skin. He led me to a table where I found, smiling broadly, my cousin Nasser.

The man's name was Ehlayyel Bejo. He was a poet. He was arrested in 1984, when he was nineteen years old, and spent seventeen years in prison. Since the revolution, he has worked for the Ministry of Culture. He and Nasser were childhood friends. But when Ehlayyel was first imprisoned, he did not know that Nasser had an uncle in the same prison, and Nasser, just like the rest of us, had no idea that Father was in Abu Salim.

'I didn't know your father before prison,' Ehlayyel said. 'I came to know him first by his voice. When one of us young prisoners was being taken to the interrogation room, your father would call out, "Boys, if you get stuck, say Jaballa Matar told you to do it." I loved him for that, because you have no idea what hearing that did for my heart. Strength at the weakest hour. Gradually he and I started exchanging letters. He wrote me many beautiful letters that I had to destroy.'

Ehlayyel Bejo and Nasser al-Tashani risked their lives to bring us the letter that shattered the myth the Egyptian authorities had constructed. And once Father was sent down into the bottomless abyss, he did not give up their names.

*

I have always wondered if it is possible to lose your father without sensing the particular moment of his death. I recall an interview on the radio with a Syrian poet whose name I have forgotten. He came to London to give a reading. He was staying at a hotel off Grosvenor Square. One afternoon, he felt the compulsion to go out into the square.

'I walked under the trees. It was a beautiful day. But I could not get rid of a desperate sadness. I longed for my mother. When I returned to my room I found a message telling me that she had just passed away.'

I remember hearing that on the radio and thinking, it makes perfect sense. Of course, I told myself, it would be impossible that I should fail to detect the moment when someone I love dies. And this thought often comforted me, particularly when hope was thin. And now that it is unimaginable that my father is alive, I am unsettled by the failure. So much happens in this world without us blinking.

Most likely, Father was killed in the massacre at Abu Salim. Several of the prisoners had told me that, although they did not see him, they had heard from others that Jaballa Matar was amongst those who were brought into the courtyard that day. Ehlayyel Bejo was taken aback by the fact that I even doubted it, but then when I asked him if he or anyone he knew saw my father that day, he said, 'No,' and then added, 'But it's obvious.' Another prisoner, who was in a cell facing the passage into the courtyard, told me, 'I can almost swear I saw him, but I can't be certain because the light wasn't good. It was very early in the morning.' It is possible that such accounts were made deliberately ambiguous in order to soften the blow. So, although it has never been confirmed, the most probable day my father's life ended was the 29th of June 1996, when he was fifty-seven and I was twenty-five.

*

Throughout all the years, all the searching and investigating I had done, I had never looked at my diary from that year. I am not a regular diarist. There are years when I have made only a handful of entries. Recently, on returning from seeing the Titian exhibition in Rome, I searched my notebooks and found the one from 1996. And there it was, an entry made on the 29th of June, the day of the massacre. It was a Saturday. I was living in the West End, some twenty minutes' walk from the National Gallery, and poor. For weeks all I ate was rice and lentils. I was always terribly anxious about money. Worry was like acid in the waking hours. But I looked as smart as I could and made a rule of not telling anyone how desperate I was. The entry reads:

'Could not get out of bed till noon. Walked to NG. Done with the Velázquez. I've switched to Manet's *Maximilian*. Never speak about money worries again. Tomorrow draw.'

The following day there is another entry. One line:

'Didn't draw.'

I read them again. There was something dizzying about the distance. I had obviously broken my rule, been complaining the night before about money. But that alone cannot explain why, being the early riser I usually am, I could not get out of bed till noon. Most of all, what sent a shiver through me was the fact that, on the day 1,270 men were executed in the prison where my father was held, I chose to switch my vigil, which by then I had been keeping for six years, to Édouard Manet's *The Execution of Maximilian*, a picture of a political execution.

The seventeenth-century Spanish painter Diego Velázquez, who had a hold on me during those years, is counted amongst the influences on the French painter Manet. It was probably this chronology of influences that had organized my decision. Nonetheless, it is unsettlingly appropriate. Manet was responding to one of the most controversial political events of his time. The French intervention in Mexico had come to a disastrous end with the execution of their installed ruler, Emperor Maximilian, in 1867. There were no photographs of the incident.

Manet had to rely on the stories he heard and the accounts he read in the papers. In the same year, he began work on several imaginings of the event. Over the next couple of years he was to complete three large paintings, an oil sketch and a lithograph depicting the fall of Maximilian. They are scattered around the world. The one at the National Gallery happens to be the most poignant, not least of all because, after the artist's death, the painting was cut up and sold in fragments. The impressionist artist Edgar Degas purchased the surviving pieces, and it was not until 1992, two years after my father's disappearance, that the National Gallery assembled them on a single canvas. Large chunks of the picture remain missing. You cannot see Maximilian – only his hand, gripped tightly by one of his generals. The firing squad is as ruthlessly focused and indifferent as the men surrounding Saint Lawrence. It would be hard to think of a painting that better evokes the inconclusive fate of my father and the men who died in Abu Salim. Learning of the fact that my unknowing 25-year-old self was guided, whether by reason or instinct, to this picture on the same day as the massacre unnerved me and has since changed my relationship to all the works of this French artist, who, somewhere in Proust's novels, is described as the painter of countless portraits of vanished models, 'models who already belonged to oblivion or to history'. Today, whenever I see a Manet, the white, his white, which is unlike any other white, cannot be a cloud, a tablecloth or a woman's dress but will always remain the white leather belts of the firing squad in *The Execution of Maximilian*.

16. The Campaign

Throughout all that has happened in the past two and a half decades since I lost my father, all the successes and failures, all the various tasks one has had to do in order to take one step this way or that, all the discoveries and missed opportunities, the falling-outs, the new loves and new friends, as I pleased some and upset others, as each discovery conducted its particular adjustment, beside all my loud and silent hours, the train of my efforts to find my father's whereabouts rolled on. It pushed its way into the dark, yielding nothing, and seeming, with every passing year, a product of its own craving. For a quarter of a century now, hope has been seeping out of me. Now I can say, I am almost free of it. All that remains are a few scattered grains.

In 2009, nineteen years into the fog, in February, the grimmest month in the English calendar, when the sheets of cloud come in two and three layers, a man telephoned. He told me that he had been a prisoner for eight years and that only recently was he released.

'I saw your father, I saw him in the Mouth of Hell,' he said. 'It was several years ago.'

'When precisely?'

'Back in 2002.'

'You saw my father in 2002?'

'Yes, 2002.'

If it were true, it would have been the only time anyone had seen my father after 1996, after the massacre.

I told him I wasn't able to speak freely and asked whether I could call him back in an hour or so. He gave me his number. Everything stopped. Everything I was doing before that moment and everything I was planning to do next vanished. I looked into the man's background. He had indeed been a political prisoner, and the prison with the macabre name did, in fact, exist. It was a high-security facility in Tripoli. I dialled the number he had given me. He answered straight away.

'How did he appear?' I asked.

'What do you mean?' the man asked.

'How did he look? His face? His health?'

'I only saw him once, and very briefly. He was frail but well.'

The words 'frail' and 'well' rumbled silently in my mouth. Hope, like water on parched earth, surged over me, heavy, drowning. It was tremendous news. Tremendous in the way a storm or a flood can be tremendous. When your father has been made to disappear for nineteen years, your desire to find him is equalled by your fear of finding him. You are the scene of a shameful private battle.

*

Human Rights Watch published the sighting in its next report, which came out on the 12th of December 2009.

The press it attracted invigorated my search. Together with several human rights organizations, journalists and writers, we launched a campaign focused on my father's case and, more broadly, human rights in Libya. We sought to make the close diplomatic ties Britain was then enjoying with the Qaddafi regime contingent on material reform in Libya. An open letter to the foreign secretary, David Miliband, was organized by the English chapter of the worldwide association of writers, PEN International. It urged the British government to:

> use its new relationship with the Libyan government to demand sincere and significant improvements in Libya's human rights record. We therefore ask the Foreign Office whether, having regard to the latest Human Rights Watch report ... in which Jaballa [Matar]'s case is documented, it will seek information from the Libyan government about the whereabouts of Jaballa and other political prisoners.

The letter was published in *The Times* on the 15th of January 2010. The more notable names amongst its 270 signatories were printed. That day, the Libyan embassy in London 'was shaking', as a member of the staff there told me. 'You caused an earthquake,' he said. The ambassador was heard shouting, 'Where the hell did this Hisham Matar descend on us from?' My mobile phone began to exhibit strange signs. It would switch off and on by itself. I became paranoid. A couple of years before, a man claiming to be a member of the Libyan secret service – who also claimed to have my 'best interests at heart' – had told me that I have a 'red light' on my head. He had said he wanted to warn me 'because you must stop. I am worried about you.' I now imagined that 'red light' growing brighter. Pathetically, I carried a knife in my pocket every time I stepped out of the flat. A shadow lingered over our hours, penetrating every room of our home.

David Miliband responded immediately. His reply was also published in *The Times*.

'Hisham and his family need to know the truth now,' he wrote. '[Jaballa Matar's disappearance] is one of a number of concerns we have about the human rights situation in Libya.'

Friends gathered around me like a grove. One built a website, another managed social media, and all opened up their address books. One friend in particular, Paul van Zyl, who had extensive experience in dealing with oppressive governments through his work with the International Center for Transitional Justice, became my closest ally and adviser. I consulted him every step of the way. I became obsessed. I lost my reticence. I was prepared to contact anyone if I thought they could help. For three months I did not write a single sentence. I hardly slept. The only thing I could read was poetry, and only a few lines at a time, and all the while the blood ran hotly in my veins. My mind became a tightly revving engine, thinking only of the next task. In rare moments of calm, when the motor would quieten down, there was a taste of the inauthentic. I could not understand it then. Was I not doing all I could? Doesn't a son have a right to know what happened to his father? But it turns out when you are looking for your father you are also looking for other things. This was why the harder I looked, the less present he became in my thoughts. It's a paradox, but my father never felt more distant than during those days when every minute was dedicated to finding him. Every week his name was mentioned at least once in a newspaper, a radio or television programme. I would remain awake for two or three days in a row, then collapse for twelve or more hours, waking up unnerved and confused, not entirely clear where I was. It was from within one such state of deep unconsciousness that I dreamt of him. He walked into the flat. The living room was exactly as it had been on that particular day: the same arrangement of papers on the table, the same wilting flowers, the same empty tea cup on the floor in front of the fireplace. He stood at the room's entrance, watching me. For some reason, he did not want to come in. He was cross about something. Eventually he spoke.

'You are not paying me enough attention,' he said.

One of the injustices involved in disappearing a person is a difficult one to describe. It turns the disappeared into an abstraction, and, because the possibility of his existing under the same sun and the same moon is a real one, it makes it hard to retain a clear picture of him. In death the hallmark fades, and not all the memorials in the world can hold back the tide of forgetting. But in life the disappeared changes in ways that are active and elaborate.

*

A few days after the open letter and David Miliband's response, the novelist Kamila Shamsie and the respected authority on international law Philippe Sands co-wrote a newspaper article in which they concluded:

> [Jaballa] Matar's initial disappearance violated international law; his continuing imprisonment without communication with the outside world violates international law; his disappearance over nearly two decades violates international law; the failure by the Libyan government to effectively investigate his case violates international law. These violations expose individuals within the Libyan government to the risk of criminal action. What this means is that Hisham Matar's rights are being violated. As a UK national he is entitled to expect the British government to intervene directly with Libya to bring the torture to an end.

The following day Ziad, who flew over for the purpose, Diana and I, and a group of our friends sat in the gallery of the House of Lords. At 2.44 p.m. the barrister and human rights advocate Lord Lester stood up and asked Her Majesty's government whether, following the Human Rights Watch report, it would seek 'information from the government of Libya about the whereabouts of Jaballa Hamed Matar'.

Hearing Father's name spoken in my adopted country's highest chamber had a vertiginous effect on me. Every time it was repeated, the feeling reoccurred. Not pride so much as a dizzying hollowness. I was certain Ziad felt it too. His eyes were perfectly still and his face was drawn back a little. I had the overwhelming urge to pull him by the hand and run out of the neo-gothic building, run till we had no strength left.

The minister of state, Baroness Kinnock, responded. She cited David Miliband's reply to the open letter and added, 'Our embassy in Tripoli has raised this with the Libyans and has asked them to investigate further.'

Several other members of the House weighed in.

Baroness Kennedy said, 'I would also be grateful if the minister could tell us whether the [British] government have sought an investigation into the massacre that took place in Abu Salim prison in 1996 ... To what extent are the government muting criticism of human rights abuses in Libya to establish trade relations, particularly on oil?'

The minister of state refuted the suggestion that 'business interests motivate our actions.'

Baroness D'Souza then stood up. 'My Lords, could the minister confirm when the case of Jaballa Matar last came up in direct discussions between the UK and Libyan governments?'

'In fact I can tell the noble Baroness that the last discussions on Jaballa Matar's case took place this weekend,' the minister of state said.

Another member, Lord Hunt, broadened the demands further, linking the UK support of a current European Union proposal to strengthen trade relations with Libyan reform. 'Would the minister answer this simple question: does she agree that the EU / Libya framework agreement must be based on meaningful progress in the areas of political and human rights reform? If she does, can we just hear an affirmative answer?'

'The answer is yes,' the minister of state said.

Another member, Lord Avebury, then spoke. 'My lords, we, too, are grateful to the foreign secretary for his statement on Jaballa Matar . . . Could the foreign secretary now publish a complete list of all the individual representations that have been made to the Libyan government together with the text of any replies that have been received?'

Peter Mandelson, who, together with Tony Blair, was the other senior member of the Labour Party who had close relations with Qaddafi's son, Seif el-Islam, was present. Throughout the proceedings, he kept his eyes on me. His expression was theatrically hard and seemed deliberately without emotion. It summed up the cynicism with which some members of the British establishment were conducting relations with the Libyan dictatorship.

After the session ended we felt bold and optimistic. None of us had expected the support to be so broad or so passionate. Lord Lester came to tell us that it was unusual for such questions, which are allotted only a few minutes for discussion, to provoke so many supporting statements. We walked out and for a few moments that afternoon I felt useful.

*

More articles appeared. BBC World Service radio was preparing a documentary on my father's disappearance. I gave countless interviews to television channels. Then something unprecedented happened. The Nobel Peace Prize winner and former archbishop of Cape Town, Desmond Tutu, issued a statement calling on Muammar Qaddafi

> to urgently clarify the fate and whereabouts of Jaballa Matar … Libya's passage from isolation to acceptance will only be complete when it has provided victims of human rights abuse with the remedies they deserve. Addressing the case of Jaballa Matar would be an excellent place to start.

Never before had an African figure of Tutu's stature publically criticized Qaddafi. Most African leaders, reliant on Libyan handouts, were shamefully servile to the dictator. One of Qaddafi's rare honourable acts was his long-term and unwavering support of the African National Congress, which made members of the South African anti-apartheid movement even less likely to speak out against human rights abuses in Libya. Back in 2002, I had sent a letter to Nelson Mandela via a friend who had played a prominent role in the anti-apartheid movement and who knew the South African president personally. In the letter I asked Mr Mandela whether, given his close ties with Qaddafi, he could enquire about my father's whereabouts and well-being. The answer, which was given to my friend, was unambiguous: 'Mandela says to never ask him such a thing again.' As it was second hand, it is impossible to be certain of the wording, but what was clear is that even a man as great as Nelson Mandela felt too indebted to Qaddafi to risk upsetting him. Such concerns were clearly not important to the archbishop. His statement gained our campaign extraordinary momentum.

I became a thorn in the side of both the Libyan and the British governments. After several requests to meet with David Miliband, I was finally granted an audience. I took with me a friend, one of the very first and most active organizers of the campaign, and Lord Lester, who had by then become a central figure in our attempts to link British–Libyan cooperation to political and human rights reform in Libya. The Foreign and Commonwealth Office building is architecturally interesting in the way that it suffers from conflicting influences. Its architect, George Gilbert Scott, was an exponent of the gothic revival, an architectural movement that dominated Britain from the mid 1700s to the mid 1800s. Augustus Pugin, one of its stars and the man behind the frenzied architecture of the Palace of Westminster, where the House of Lords is housed, was an inspiration for George Gilbert Scott. But the brief for the FCO building constrained Scott. It demanded an Italianate design, one deriving its influences from sixteenth-century Italian renaissance architecture. The result is a strangely contradictory building: Italianate bones; eclectic decorations that evoke a sense of British colonial romanticism; and – in the overbearing weight of the interiors, their determination to control the light – the temperament and atmosphere of gothic revival architecture. Like the ministry it houses, the building also wants to be elsewhere. Walking through its long corridors, Lord

Lester began telling my friend and me about the various idiosyncrasies of the institution. He seemed anxious. He walked up alongside me.

'One of the things he is going to ask you is why you didn't come to him sooner. The government is not happy with all the press,' Lord Lester said. A few steps later he said, 'Now, remember to compliment him. You can compliment him on the Labour Party's human rights record.'

'I can't possibly do that,' I said.

'Well, you must think of something.'

'Actually, I have,' I said. 'I was going to compliment him on his father.' I had read the prominent sociologist Ralph Miliband's book *The State in Capitalist Society*.

'What? You mean that Marxist?' Lord Lester said. 'For all you know he might hate his father.'

'Even so, a man who hates his father likes other men complimenting him.'

'I think you should think of something else,' Lord Lester said.

We were led into a waiting room, and a couple of minutes later taken to David Miliband's office. He met us at the door. He was warm and jovial. Made some joke that I now can't remember. The office was a large room with arched windows, the high ceiling gilded, the walls papered in dark green with a running motif in gold. There was a large painting above the fireplace of a regal-looking Indian man holding a sword. Also present was the Foreign Office's Libya desk officer, Declan Byrne. We sat on red leather armchairs. David Miliband asked me to take the one beside him. I took note of his exceptionally hairless hands. Lord Lester was right. The first thing Miliband asked was why I hadn't come to him sooner.

'Before all the noise,' he said, and gestured with his hand, smiling affably.

I didn't think it worthwhile to remind him that I had made several previous requests for this meeting. All I said was, 'But the only reason I am here is because of the noise.'

He was obviously an intelligent and charismatic man, but it was at this point, perhaps in part provoked by the conversation with Lord Lester, that I decided not to bother complimenting him on his father.

The only commitment we came away with was that the British ambassador in Libya would make fortnightly presentations regarding my father to the Libyan government. This was significant. The pressure would be sustained. Walking me out, David Miliband placed his hand on my shoulder.

'So tell me,' he said. 'Are you British now?'

'Yes.'

'Good man. Excellent. So you're one of us.'

Was he patronizing me? Perhaps not. Perhaps it was the genuine warm confederacy of a fellow-Brit. Or, then again, maybe it was the impatient, political, bullying pragmatism of power towards a person of mixed identities, a man whose preoccupations do not fit neatly inside the borders of one country, and so perhaps what Miliband was really saying was, 'Come on, you're British now; forget about Libya.'

*

Every couple of weeks I would contact the Libya desk at the Foreign Office. Several times I went there, signed in at security, and was led through the corridors to a boardroom right on the top floor to meet with Declan Byrne and his colleagues. When the Conservatives won the elections, the new foreign secretary, William Hague, decided, according to the FCO, to 'carry on with the current policy'. They confirmed Hague's commitment to these fortnightly representations. At every meeting I asked if these presentations yielded anything, and every time I was told, 'No.' I believed that by taking what an unwilling partner was giving me, even if it was insincere, I would be able to maintain the momentum. Once it became obvious, I thought, that these presentations were useless, I could press for a different strategy. That was how my brain worked then; now I think differently.

*

Besides Tony Blair and Peter Mandelson, there were many other influential figures within the British establishment who were closely associated with the Libyan regime. We wanted to make those involved in business with the Libyan dictatorship aware of the case. The financier Nathaniel Rothschild was friends with Seif el-Islam. A friend of mine knew his father, Jacob Rothschild, and offered to introduce me. I had never met a man so steeped in power. You could feel it emanating from the walls of his office. Lord Rothschild, who, I learnt throughout our meeting, had served for two years as an adviser to the Libyan Investment Authority, began by telling me of various people he knew who were connected to the Libyan dictatorship. He spoke about them with interest and curiosity. I thought, for men like him, the world must seem an amusing affair. I handed him a file on my father's case.

'Given the close relations British government and businesses have with the Libyan regime,' I told him, 'it is a golden opportunity for Britain to play a constructive role in the betterment of the lives of the Libyan people. This case is a good place to start.'

Lord Rothschild said he was willing to help. He said he had met Seif el-Islam on more than one occasion. 'I will ask Nat to speak to Seif.'

I walked out of his office, took the shortest route to the National Gallery and stood in front of Canaletto's *The Stonemason's Yard*.

Several days later Jacob Rothschild wrote to say that Seif el-Islam was in London. He included a mobile number and said that he was expecting my call.

17. The Dictator's Son

Ever since 2004, when Tony Blair went to Libya and relations were normalized, some Libyan friends had urged me to make contact with Seif el-Islam. It was known that on more than one occasion, as Libya's image was undergoing a facelift, he had released political prisoners. And recently, in 2009, he had done the seemingly impossible: he managed to extract Abdelbaset al-Megrahi – a Libyan intelligence officer convicted of 270 counts of murder for the bombing of Pan Am Flight 103 over Lockerbie – from the clutches of the Scottish justice system. When the plane landed in Tripoli, Seif stepped out victoriously, holding the hand of al-Megrahi up in the air. The wind filled Seif's sleeve, ballooning the fabric. Shortly after this, Seif bought a house in Hampstead. For several days after I heard the news, I had to drive away thoughts of knocking on his door and shooting him.

In 2003, when I was living in Paris, and a few days after I came close to jumping off a bridge, I sat down and wrote Seif el-Islam the sort of letter I had been writing for years to Libyan and Egyptian authorities, detailing the known facts of my father's case and asking them to clarify his fate. Over the years I have written nearly 300 such letters. I have not once received a response. One day we staged a demonstration in front of the Egyptian embassy in London. The policeman handed our letter to the young Egyptian diplomat standing at the entrance of the embassy. The diplomat held the envelope high above his head, so we could all see him slowly rip it in two. It was not so much his action that remained with me but the expression on his face, vehemence that told of a curious mixture of loathing and shame. That became the face of all those who never answered my letters. I never wrote to Seif again. But now, seven years later and at the height of the campaign, I was a desperate man, willing to talk to the devil in order to find out if my father was alive or dead. That was how I was then; I am no longer like that now.

*

I dialled the number Lord Rothschild sent me. There was no answer. I left a message. Ten minutes later the phone rang, showing a different number. I heard a man's voice uttering the typical run of hollow platitudes, even more meaningless than usual, for he didn't leave time for a reply. Then he said, 'I am Seif.'

I introduced myself and asked for a meeting.

He said I would be contacted with a time and a place.

In the evening a man called and said, 'I'm Rajab el-Laiyas.' He said it as though he expected me to know of him. 'We'll meet tomorrow at 5 p.m. at the Jumeirah. You know it?'

When I hung up, I thought, anything could happen. I could discover my father's fate or be kidnapped like him. And I recalled those dark few minutes at the edge of the Pont d'Arcole in Paris. What had taken me there was discovering that, although I was living with the woman I loved and, for the first time ever, was able to dedicate most of my time to writing, and the sun shone most days and we ate well, the only relief I could think of from the pain maintained by every ticking second would come from being in that same 'noble palace' in Abu Salim with my father.

I telephoned Ziad in Cairo. I asked when he could get here. He took the night flight and was at my door by the following morning. We smoked a lot, we drank endless cups of coffee, and we tried to prepare. We ran through all the possible scenarios: will they ask us up to a room or will we meet in the lobby, or will they ask us to accompany them elsewhere, and what might their strategy be, and how ought we to respond? I notified key figures in our campaign of the time and place of the meeting. Diana was to wait at a nearby café with a list of numbers to call in case we didn't come back.

The Jumeirah Carlton Tower Hotel is in Knightsbridge. The only thing I knew about it was that long ago, when it had a different name, the Peruvian novelist Mario Vargas Llosa and the Mexican poet Octavio Paz used to meet there. We arrived ten minutes early and took one of the round tables for four in the café in the lobby. It was to one side, with a good view of the entrance. I am not sure if my recollections of the hotel lobby are accurate or if they have been affected by my state at the time. Either way, this is how I remember it. In the lounge, heavy Arab businessmen sat in gigantic armchairs. Suited English architects or developers leant over them, pointing to spread sheets and architectural plans. The more these prospecting Englishmen bent over, the tighter their neckties became and the redder their faces grew.

Although neither of us felt like it, Ziad and I ordered tea.

A woman who looked a little embarrassed occupied the centre of the lobby, plucking away at a harp. Her skill was clear, but she had obviously been instructed to stick to instrumentals of well-known pop songs. She was now in the opening bars of 'Yesterday' by the Beatles. We spotted the television preacher Amr Khaled sitting with a group of admirers. At several other tables around the lobby, high-class prostitutes sat in pairs, sipping wine. They looked like artificial flowers. After a marathon of popular tunes, the harpist allowed herself a brief diversion. One of Bach's *Goldberg Variations*. Number 7, I think. It lasted about a minute.

An hour after the agreed time, a group of men in jeans and T-shirts, looking more like a hip-hop band than a security outfit, walked quickly towards our table. Seif had chosen his entourage carefully. With him he had Mohammad al-Hawni, a 65-year-old lawyer based in Rome, from where he served Libyan–Italian business interests. We dubbed him the Intellectual, as his main purpose was to impress upon us that some of Seif's aides read books. The rest were bodyguards – one of whom, Seif was keen to point out, was a member of our tribe. Seif sat opposite me, the Intellectual opposite Ziad, and the bodyguards took the table behind us.

Ziad donned his usual air of confidence and affability. I feared this taxed him more than the role I played taxed me. He asked the men what they would like to drink and whether they frequented this place.

'I suppose it's your hangout?' Ziad said in English, and smiled.

Seif then asked, 'Who is the writer?'

Ziad told him I was.

'You are the writer?' Seif asked again.

'Yes,' I said.

'Is that all you do?'

'I am afraid so,' I said.

'What, you mean all you do is write?'

'Precisely.'

'You don't do anything else?'

'I try not to,' I said.

'You are a wonderful writer,' Mohammad al-Hawni put in. 'A great talent. We are very proud of you.'

'I'm surprised you read me, given that my books are banned in Libya.'

'No, no, no,' the Intellectual said. '*In the Country of Men*, right? I read it. I read it in Italian. Excellent book. Do you have anything else on the way? Hurry up, we are waiting.'

All this tedious nonsense had a serious purpose. It was to figure out how on earth this mere writer was able to rustle up such 'noise', as Miliband put it. How did he manage to marshal senior members of the House of Lords, the Foreign Office, Nobel laureates, international legal authorities, human rights groups and NGOs? Is he a spy? Why is he not tempted by money? How – the question power always asks – can we get to him?

One of Seif's bodyguards handed him a phone. 'Excuse me,' Seif said and took the call.

'Excellent book,' Mohammad al-Hawni whispered. Then, a little while later, '*In the Country of Men.*'

Just as Seif was ending his call, Ziad looked at me and smiled his mischievous smile. He said, loud enough for the others to hear, 'See this fine young man?'

'What did you say?' Seif asked as soon as he hung up.

'I was just saying what a fine young man you are.'

Notwithstanding these bizarre exchanges, the meeting started well. Ziad set out the bare facts of the case and gave a brief history of our long struggle to get information. Seif broke with the official line. Instead of denying Father's abduction and incarceration, he confirmed that our father had been taken to Libya.

'This is a highly complicated case,' he said. 'It involves the Egyptian secret services and the Libyan secret services. It would bring me a lot of trouble, but I am prepared to do it. I promise you both that I will look into it and bring you all the facts, minute by minute, of what took place, whether it is good news or bad news.'

'Even if he is dead,' Mohammad al-Hawni put in.

That was the first hint.

'You can do with it as you please,' Seif continued. 'I am prepared to publish it myself. I'll get a full page in a newspaper and print it there,' he said, as though it was a dare. 'I want to close the file.'

Then he spoke of how dangerous my father was to the Libyan regime.

'If you are so confident,' I said, 'you should have put him on trial.'

'What happened was stupid,' he said, which implied

that there was another, 'cleverer' way of making him disappear.

'Look,' I said, 'you and your father might disagree with my father's politics, but do you doubt his patriotism?'

'No,' Seif said.

'Then shame on you.' I wasn't sure what I was doing. Part of me wanted to test him, to see if, like his father, he had a fiery temper. 'You took one of Libya's finest and took him in a cowardly way, then pretended no one saw. A man who devoted himself to his country and whose father before him fought to liberate Libya from the Italians. It's not so much stupid as criminal.'

Then Ziad, softening the tone, said, 'But, listen, we are hopeful. We want to give you a chance to limit the damage, the ongoing damage this is causing our family.'

'What do you do in Cairo?' Seif asked Ziad.

'I am an industrialist. I make clothes.'

'So you have factories?'

'Yes.'

'You make clothes – what sort of clothes?'

'For the American market, mainly.'

'Why don't you return? If you want to do business, we will help you. Libya is your country. We want you to break this barrier.'

'We can't talk of that now,' Ziad said. 'Besides, I can barely make my business succeed standing still, let alone by moving it.'

Then Seif looked at me and with an impatient tone said, 'What do you want if he is dead?'

That was the second hint.

'We want to know when, where and how it happened,' I said. 'We want the body in order to bury it in our own way, so we can have our funeral, and then we want accountability. You talk of "closing the file": this is how you do it.' I was taken aback by the cold mechanical tone in my voice. It was as if I knew then that none of this would happen.

'Understood,' Seif said.

'And what if he is alive?' Ziad asked.

Seif paused, rocking his leg. 'No, no, no,' he said. 'The question is: what if he is dead?'

And that was the third hint. Father is dead.

'Yes, but if he is alive?' Ziad persisted.

'Either way, I will get you all the facts,' Seif said, then repeated what would become his refrain in our future conversations, which lasted thirteen months: 'I want to close the file.'

I pressed him to commit to a date by which he would provide us with the information.

'Soon,' he said.

'Weeks or months?'

'Weeks, weeks,' he said. Then he said again, 'But return. Libya is your country. We want you to break this barrier.'

'This "barrier" you speak of,' Ziad said, 'is not due to shyness or timidity. We love our country. We have sacrificed a great deal for it. But any talk of us going back cannot take place before three things happen.'

'What are they?' Seif asked.

'Knowing the fate of our father, and securing the release of our two uncles, Mahmoud Matar and Hmad

Khanfore, and our two cousins, Ali and Saleh Eshnay-quet. They have been political prisoners for the same period of time. The court has already issued their release, yet they remain in prison. Uncle Mahmoud is very ill and has been refused proper medical care.'

'OK. What else do you want?' Seif said.

'Our family home in Tripoli was stolen by a member of the regime. We want it returned.'

Seif slapped the table and said, 'Consider it done.'

When Seif and the others stood up to leave, Moham-mad al-Hawni lingered behind. He put one hand on my shoulder and the other on Ziad's shoulder.

'I want you to have faith in God. You are grown men now and must prepare yourselves for the worst.'

'When did it happen?' I asked.

He put his hands up. 'I don't know anything for certain. I am just saying ...'

'We are not here for advice or sympathy,' I told him. 'We want facts.'

'And Seif told you he will get you the facts.'

*

Ziad and I left the hotel. We avoided the main road and took the side streets towards Sloane Square and the café where Diana was waiting. It was a cold night. We walked slowly.

'That was one of the hardest things I've ever had to do,' Ziad said.

I felt responsible. I questioned the wisdom of putting

us through it all, of placing us at the same table with the son of the man who killed our father.

'Father is dead,' I said.

'But you don't know that.'

'It's fucking obvious, isn't it?'

Why this need to push his face in it? It was as if my desire for Ziad to accept it and my irritation at his stubborn denial was the self-same need and irritation I had towards my own refusal, for I too worked, as we walked away from that cursed hotel, with my small and moronic engine of hope, searching for how it could not be true.

When Diana saw us cross the road, she ran out of the café. She knew immediately that the news was not good. None of us could stand still. We hailed a cab and all sat in the back seat. We reached home. We stood in front of the house for a minute or so, then decided to keep on walking. We ended up at the local restaurant. One of my closest friends telephoned, and a few minutes later he was walking into the restaurant. He looked at me consolingly, with eyes that read 'How can I help?' This, I thought to myself, must be how mourners look at the bereaved. We ordered and then my phone rang, showing an unknown number. It was Mohammad al-Hawni, calling exactly an hour after our meeting. I walked out on to the street.

'I'm so pleased we met,' he said. 'I just want you and your brother to prepare yourselves for the worst.'

'Look, Mr al-Hawni, please don't feel the need to prepare us. We are not children. It has been twenty years. You cannot ask me to give up hope until we know the facts.' As

I said this I could hear, in the night air, my tired small engine whirring in the background.

'Do you think if Seif knew that your father was alive he would not tell you?' he asked.

'So Seif knows?' I asked.

'Of course he knows.'

*

One month after our meeting, Seif called one evening at 7 p.m. I was on the bus, heading to the Wigmore Hall, late for a concert.

'I want you to think of me as a brother and a friend,' he said, and when I didn't say anything, he added, 'I see you as a friend and a brother.'

I got off at the next stop and walked into a quiet street.

'I really think we can be good friends, you and I,' he said.

'People can't choose their history,' I told him, hearing that same cold mechanical tone return. 'And if two men with as disparate histories as yours and mine can come to regard one another as friends and, who knows, perhaps even as brothers, that is something that will no doubt go some way towards healing our country.'

'Good,' he said. 'Good. Like I told you and your brother, I am determined to close the file. But in order for us to progress to the next step, I will need you to write down what you and your brother told me. Exactly how you told the story when we met. You send me this and I will let you know the next step.'

'But is there nothing you can tell me now?'

'No, nothing.'

'But I know that you know.'

'I do. I know what happened to your father, but I can't tell you until I have all the facts.'

'This is very difficult. Can't you at least tell me if he is alive or dead?'

'Wait until I have the facts.'

I returned home and emailed him the information that same evening.

*

It was around those days that I got a call from an acquaintance, a Libyan diplomat stationed in New York, saying that a colleague of his, Tarek al-Abady, based at the Libyan embassy in London, wanted to speak to me. I recognized the name. Tarek al-Abady had attended the first reading I gave from my first book, back in March 2006, three months before the book was due to be published, when hardly anyone knew of it or of me. The reading was at the Irish Cultural Centre in Hammersmith. Walking there, I had thought of Samuel Beckett. I thought of him because the Irish Cultural Centre was close to Riverside Studios, where, in the 1980s, the Irish playwright had come from Paris to rehearse *Waiting for Godot*. My friend David Gothard, who was then the artistic director of Riverside Studios, told me once that the moment Beckett arrived in London he felt dangerously close to home and instructed David, 'Under no circumstance, not even for a funeral, can you allow me to take myself to Dublin.' I admired Beckett's stubbornness. When I arrived at the Irish Cultural Centre, I saw three figures from the embassy sitting in the front row. Tarek al-Abady was one of them, and introduced himself as the cultural attaché. As soon as I stopped reading, one of them put his hand up in the air. 'Why did you set your book in Libya? We want you to write about life here in London.' A few days later a report was sent to Tripoli and my book was banned.

I had seen Tarek al-Abady again. I was walking westward on Knightsbridge and he in the opposite direction, towards Hyde Park Corner and the Libyan embassy.

'Mr Hisham,' he called out. 'What a pleasure. Please, come honour us at the embassy. Anything you need, just ask.'

I was in a foul mood. 'Anything I need?' I said sharply. 'Well, let's see, what might I need from you people? Oh, yes, I remember now. The same thing I have been asking for since 1990. What did you do with my father?'

I wondered what now, four years later, Tarek al-Abady wanted. We agreed to meet at my private club. I chose the venue because it allowed me to ask for the list of names of those he would be bringing with him.

'It'll just be me,' he said.

'I don't know how you normally dress, but the club's dress code is jacket and tie.'

'I am a diplomat,' he snapped. 'I always wear a suit.'

I asked the club to prepare a room all the way up on the top floor. Instead of taking the lift, I took him up the stairs. When we reached the top he was breathless. We sat down and for some reason I took note of the time. He started by telling me that he was from 'a good family'. Then he relayed his soliloquy.

'I want you to know, and may God be my witness, that my number-one ambition in life, more than anything else, is to be your friend. I admire you and have always wondered – if you allow me to be honest – what is stopping you from coming back to your country. Libya isn't Qaddafi's. It doesn't belong to him or his family. It belongs to you. Come back. Let us honour you. You've let others honour you. Countries around the world have given you awards and prizes; let us do the same. We want to give you prizes too. And if you want to engage in business, you own a share in Libya's wealth ...' and so on.

These introductory comments lasted for over twenty minutes before he said, 'I have been sent to you by Seif el-Islam Qaddafi and Abuzed Dorda.'

Abuzed Dorda was the director of the Mukhabarat el-Jamahiriya, the intelligence services under Qaddafi.

'First of all,' Tarek continued, 'allow me to vouch for them both. I swear, and may God be my witness, when Seif walks into the embassy, he is concerned about each individual and asks us all, not sparing one, if we are well and whether there is anything we need, anything. As for Abuzed Dorda, he is as decent as they come. They are asking one question and one question only: "What does Hisham Matar want?"'

'How funny,' I said. 'I spoke to Seif only the other day. He could've asked me himself.'

'Well, to be honest,' Tarek al-Abady corrected himself, 'it was more Abuzed Dorda who sent me. And he tells you if there is anything you need, anything at all, all you have to do is ask.' And he repeated, 'We want to honour you. We want to give you prizes. Come to Libya and allow us to give you prizes like other people have done.'

'So Dorda sent you?'

'Exactly,' he said.

'Therefore you are a member of the Mukhabarat, then?'

'Absolutely not,' he said, indignant. 'I am a diplomat. I am a career diplomat.'

'OK, fine. Please thank Mr Dorda. Tell him I appreciate his concern and that Hisham Matar is perplexed as to why Abuzed Dorda is perplexed as to what it is Hisham Matar wants. It is what I have been asking for for twenty years: what have you done with my father? As for prizes, I dislike attention. I am also terrible with money. If I have ten pounds in my pocket I cannot wait to spend it.'

'I give you my word,' he said. 'I will tell him exactly what you said and ask him, and ask others too, about your father.'

As we descended the stairs, he began to feign sympathy.

'To be honest, it is very difficult working for this regime. It's a headache. So many problems to resolve.'

Then he told me with pride that he was awarded his London post in return for the 'clean-up' he had done in Switzerland following the scandal Qaddafi's son Hannibal caused there. Hannibal had beaten his servants in a hotel in Geneva so badly that they had had to be rushed to hospital. The authorities arrested him. In retaliation, the father detained two Swiss businessmen who happened to be in Libya at the time. The Swiss dropped the charges and allowed Hannibal to leave the country. Qaddafi refused to release the two Swiss nationals and still had them in a prison in Tripoli at this time.

'What a saga,' Tarek said. 'But thanks be to God, it all ended well.'

*

Two weeks after I had emailed Seif the information he requested, he telephoned at midnight.

'I will email you today developments and the next step,' he said.

It had been six weeks since our initial meeting. In the hope of focusing his mind, I said, 'The twentieth anniversary of the abduction of my father comes up in two weeks, on the 12th of March. Would you commit to providing the information before then?'

He sighed. 'I'll try.'

'I understand the complexities involved, but it is something that needs to be resolved urgently,' I said. I could feel my body stiffen.

'It is burdensome,' he said.

'Yes, and the greater burden is on this side of the fence. A proper resolution will be of great benefit.'

'I will get you news before the 12th,' he said.

*

I didn't hear from him for a week. Then Mohammed Ismail, Seif's personal secretary, wrote to me.

> *Dear Hisham*
>
> *It would be better that you talk about the facts in public or publish it, because it's very sensitive that we raise it. When you do, we will reply. The part concerning your father after his arrival to Libya, we will give you access to that information. To save face this is the best way out.*
>
> *Regards,*
> *Mohammed*

The email articulated the problematic role Seif el-Islam Qaddafi occupied in Libyan public life. He was a representative of the regime – the 'we' here is the regime, and the 'face' that is to be saved is also that of the regime – but he had no official role and therefore, when it suited him, he played the part of the independent reformer.

Immediately on receiving the email, I called Mohammed Ismail. He said they needed me to make a public announcement in one of the English papers mentioning the role Egypt had played in the abduction. 'In order to save face,' he repeated.

'This has been done already, on countless occasions, and most recently a week ago,' I said.

'I didn't know this,' he said.

'Have you not seen the press?'

'No,' he said.

I suspected this to be disingenuous and later that suspicion was confirmed. Given how closely connected Seif was to the embassy in London and how perturbed the embassy was by all the media, it is impossible that he and his aides did not know.

'I'll send you a selection of articles and interviews on the subject that detail Egypt's involvement,' I said.

*

Three days later, on the evening of Friday, the 5th of March, a week before the twentieth anniversary of my father's disappearance, Mohammed Ismail telephoned.

'I am coming to London tomorrow. Let's meet.'

I telephoned my friend Paul van Zyl. We went through all the possible scenarios. 'If at any point during the meeting you want to call me, I'll be by the phone,' he told me.

I decided not to tell Ziad. I didn't want to trouble him and get him to make the same rushed journey again. And I also wanted to reserve the option of keeping whatever terrible news Mohammed Ismail was coming to tell me to myself for a little while; then I could worry about how to break it to my family.

I couldn't sleep that night. Mother, Ziad and I had planned to be together in a couple of days to mark the date of Father's disappearance. We had no idea how one ought to commemorate such an occasion. I could not travel to Cairo because, since the publication of my first novel, it was no longer deemed safe for me to go there. So we settled on Nairobi, the city where Mother spent part of the year. I couldn't imagine having to inform her that

Father was dead. I spoke the words out loud to see how they might sound. I didn't know if I could do it. But if I knew for certain that he was dead, I would have no choice but to tell her.

Mohammed Ismail and I agreed to meet at 3 p.m. the following day. I didn't think it was wise to go alone. I called one of my closest friends whom I knew would be good under pressure. He and I met midway. My friend is an Englishman who doesn't speak a word of Arabic. I told him to pretend he did.

'Whenever I look at you,' I said, 'just nod in agreement.'

We arrived on time, and, as had happened with my first meeting with Seif, we were kept waiting for an hour. This time it was at the lobby of the InterContinental Park Lane Hotel, one of a number of London hotels purchased with Libyan Investment Authority money under the name of one of Seif's close associates. I had no idea what Mohammed Ismail looked like. Then a stocky figure walked out of one of the lifts and came towards us. We shook hands. I did not introduce my friend. I somehow thought that the more mysterious he seemed to Mohammed Ismail the better. Mohammed placed two mobile phones on the coffee table. He began by telling me of his family. His wife and child were living in London. He had named his son Hannibal.

'After Seif's brother. I love Hannibal. Oh, Hannibal is great,' he said. Mohammed Ismail then told me of his late father-in-law. 'He knew your father. They were in the military together. After the revolution my father-in-law was arrested, like your father, but was not released for another eighteen years.'

I thought of a man who had to live his last days with a grandson named after the son of the man who had incarcerated him. I remembered what Sarah Hamoud, who used to run the Libya desk at Amnesty International, once told me: 'There is no country where the oppressed and the oppressor are so intertwined as in Libya.'

Then Mohammed Ismail said, 'I have come specially to see you. I took the private jet.'

'Before you tell me what you came here to tell me,' I told Mohammed, 'I just want to remind you that we were promised the full details.'

'No, no, no,' he said. 'I am not here to tell you any news. I am here because Seif asks that you give an interview to an Egyptian journalist who writes for *Asharq al-Awsat*. We want you to tell him what happened. Then you are to write a letter to President Hosni Mubarak saying the same. When you have done this, we will supply you with the information.'

'But all this has been done. I have written countless letters to the Egyptian president and, as you saw from my email, many of my articles on the subject have already been published in the Egyptian press, clearly stating the role Egypt played in the crime.'

'I know. But we want you to do it again. You can speak to the journalist now. He's waiting by the phone. Do this and tomorrow or at the most the day after you will have everything in your hands.'

I felt exasperated. 'OK,' I said. 'Let's do it.'

He searched in his two phones for the number of the

journalist. After a long silence, he said, as if it were an afterthought, 'Why don't you come to Libya?'

'One day,' I said.

'Seif wants you to work with us. Come, work with us.'

What better confirmation of the regime's transformation than the son of a dissident working with the son of the dictator? So this is why Mohammed was telling me his little story about his father-in-law, I thought. Seif has purchased so many people that he must have thought he could surely buy me, have me cross over and, who knows, one day I might even name my son after him.

'Come work with us,' Mohammed Ismail repeated.

'I already have a job,' I said.

He couldn't find the number. He left his two mobile phones on the coffee table and went up to his room to search for it. I was sure the telephones lay there recording. My friend pulled me away from the table.

'What did he tell you?' When I told him he said, 'Don't do it. Ask for an hour to think it over. You won't lose anything. Call Paul.'

I dialled Paul's number. He answered immediately. I quickly briefed him and he said, 'Ask for some time. This way you can look into the journalist: who he is, what his record is like, et cetera.'

But I was a thirsty man. All I could think of was the prospect of finally possessing certainty over the one question that had occupied me for the past two decades and possessing it by tomorrow or, at the most, the day after. The word 'after' was like a black hole in my thoughts.

When Mohammed Ismail returned, I wrote down the

name and telephone number of the journalist. 'I am not sure I can do this,' I said. 'All that you are asking me to do has already been done. I don't understand why I am being required to further expose myself and my family in Cairo.'

'Seif personally guarantees your family's safety. No one will touch them in Egypt.'

'You know he can't guarantee that. Look, give me a few hours to think it over. In the meantime, tell Seif my reservations and that what he is asking for has already been done countless times.'

*

My enquiries about the Egyptian journalist all confirmed that he was in the pocket of Seif el-Islam. The head of Human Rights Watch in Cairo told me, 'You cannot trust him to print what you say. It's a trap.'

A couple of days later, as I was preparing to fly to Nairobi, I sent Seif an email, copying Mohammed. In it I mentioned again the names of the Egyptian newspapers that had reprinted my articles on the subject, detailing Egyptian involvement, and told them that any action that was now required had to come from them.

'We have suffered too much injustice to be asked now to go out on a limb. This is your chance to address our suffering and limit the damage done. Provide us with the truth.'

I was angry, but I was also relieved I would not have to tell my mother bad news.

18. The Good Manners of Vultures

My plane landed in Nairobi in the evening. Mother and I had supper in her small flat and sat up chatting until midnight. She lived here for part of the year because she has always loved the nature and also on account of her brother, Uncle Soleiman, who has, for several decades now, made Kenya his home. Her flat had the playful, noncommittal air of a holiday home. We fell asleep. Then Mother got up at 2 a.m. I heard her make coffee. Then she started baking bread. An hour later she went to the airport to collect Ziad. By around 5 a.m. she was back with Ziad, who came to me in bed and kissed me five or six times on the same cheek.

A little while later he was lying beside me. Mother took the sofa.

'But how will you sleep like this?' Ziad told her.

'Don't you worry,' she said. 'Do you need pyjamas?'

'No.'

After a few seconds, 'Do you need pyjamas?' she asked again.

'Awful time to arrive,' Ziad said. 'Neither morning nor night. This is what the English call "the grave hour".'

'How morbid,' Mother said. 'Don't they also call certain jobs that? "Graveyard jobs"?'

'Grave hour,' Ziad repeated.

Then we all tried to sleep. But Mother couldn't stop. She asked more questions about the flight, whether he needed pyjamas, whether we were cold and whether she should bring out the blanket. She misses us. Each one of us misses us. Maybe one day we will live in the same country again.

After a long silence passed I got up quietly in the dark and went to her.

'Go sleep next to Ziad,' I whispered.

'No,' she said.

'Let's please not argue and wake him.'

'OK,' she said. 'I have an idea.'

I knew what she was going to do and I let her do it. I went to the bathroom and when I returned she was already lying on the cushions on the floor. I sat on the terracotta tiles beside her.

'I am not moving until you go to the bed,' I said.

She got up.

'I've already turned over the pillow,' I said.

'OK, but you didn't have to do that,' she said. 'Do you need another pillow?'

'No,' I said.

'I'll get you one,' she said, and gently laid one beside me. I could feel its cool white form.

I realized that I was lying in a draught. I waited until both of their breaths turned deep and slow, then I pulled the cushions to one side.

*

When I felt the sun pressing against the curtains, I got up. Mother and Ziad were fast asleep. I got dressed and slipped out.

The earth in this country is like an inkwell. It stains every bare foot, car tyre and tree trunk a reddish brown. All else is lush green. The sky above is close and vivid. The sun is nearly audible.

When they arrived at the café they were both smiling. We spent the rest of the morning sipping passion fruit juice by the swimming pool. The trees surrounding the pool were taller than minarets. Their canopies had the effect of the vaulted ceiling of a theatre. When we spoke, we spoke about the beauty of this country, or the beauty of Ziad's children, or teased one another about a new shirt, a funky pair of sunglasses. Then we took pictures of one another.

It was clear that none of us was quite sure what we were supposed to do. Nairobi was the first place we came to when we fled Libya back in 1979. Our first place of exile. And here we were, burdening it again with the task of consoling us.

By the afternoon Mother had left. Ziad and I remained by the pool. The sun was strong. We moved beneath the sheer and translucent canopy of one of the tall trees. Its shade was as thin and even as silk on the skin. An eagle that we had seen hovering high above landed on one of the branches. It slowly folded its wings and, as if in response, the surrounding leaves shimmered. The bird was out of scale, too large even for this high tree.

We neither heard nor saw anything before a branch

crashed on the side table between Ziad's lounger and mine. It shattered my mobile phone, which I was obsessively carrying around. As I collected the various parts of the phone from the ground, I wondered whether another branch was silently racing down towards my brother or me. The waiter rushed towards us, apologized and proceeded to move our things to another pair of loungers in the sun, outside the influence of the tree.

'It could have killed us,' Ziad said.

I was busy putting the phone back together. I turned it on and stared at it until the screen lit up.

'It wasn't very big,' I said.

'Yes, but it was unexpected. A few centimetres this way or that and ...' When I didn't complete his sentence, he said, 'No?'

'Yes,' I said. 'It could have.'

One of the bathers, who saw what happened, spread her towel beneath the same tree and lay there, her shiny body terribly exposed.

'Do you think we ought to warn her?' Ziad said.

'Well, she saw it,' I said.

'Still,' he said.

Neither of us moved. The heavy eagle was still roaming the canopy. After a long silence, and within the privacy of our own thoughts, each of us seemed to have accepted that going to warn a half-naked woman we didn't know about a danger she was aware of might seem intrusive or overbearing. And her confidence was alluring; we had both registered this. Perhaps had things been different, Ziad and I could have displayed a similar coolness of mind and remained in our places, certain that such a rare occurrence as a branch crashing to the ground was unlikely to repeat itself.

I watched the eagle.

'I don't understand why eagles are so revered,' I said. 'America puts it on its dollar, we Arabs admire it, but, if you think about it, when you consider how eagles live, they are treacherous.'

'They are strong and proud,' Ziad said.

'Strong, proud and treacherous,' I said. 'They attack the young when the mother is away.'

'They are fast, have amazing precision and, unlike vultures, they eat only what they hunt,' Ziad said.

'Vultures are far more admirable,' I said.

'But how can you say that?' Ziad said.

And just when I was about to speak again, to say something about the good manners of vultures, how they do not attack unless certain that the victim is dead, I decided I didn't actually care about the subject. My mind went instead to a poem Father used to recite about the pride of eagles, and a photograph I keep of him looking into the eyes of an eagle perched on his arm. Then I wondered if the eagle above was our father. Perhaps this was why it sent a branch precisely on to my bloody phone. I didn't tell Ziad this, because I didn't want him to think that I believed Father was dead. He feared I knew more than I was saying, that Mohammed Ismail had told me something definitive and I was keeping it to myself so as not to break his heart and Mother's. The truth was, at that moment I didn't believe Father to be dead. But the truth was also that I didn't believe him to be alive either.

*

The following day, on the eve of the anniversary, I had a missed call from a number that began with the area code +55. I looked it up: +55 was the code for Brazil. I dialled the number and Mohammed Ismail answered.

'How's Brazil?' I said.

'How do you know we are in Brazil?' he asked suspiciously.

'The code.'

'Ah, OK,' he said. 'I spoke to Seif and he said you have to do it.'

'Did he see my email?'

'What email?'

'I sent you an email explaining my reasons further and stating that this issue has already been written about in Egypt recently. *Al-Dustour* newspaper published a big piece on it only a couple of weeks ago.'

'OK, we will look at the email and call you back.'

*

On the evening of the anniversary, we gathered in Mother's place. Uncle Soleiman joined us. Mother had spent the afternoon wrapping grapevine leaves and now they were laid out on a circular platter in the middle of the table along with her bread. We ate until it became hard to breathe, then we moved on to the sofa and lit cigarettes. Suddenly the reason for our reunion was unavoidable. And this was how we commemorated it. We told and retold the story of how it had happened. Each time one of us remembered a new detail. Then we told other stories, tributaries to the main one, stories that led away and then back to the same event. We were the witnesses hovering around the scene of a crime. And, as these retellings offered no comfort, we went on until 3 a.m. A couple of days later, each one of us would be in a different country. Over the following days we called each other every day, sometimes more than once.

19. The Speech

I heard back from Mohammed Ismail ten days later.

'Seif says you have to do it. You must do it. Do it and we will see if it would be possible to provide you with the information.'

'Look, you can't keep repeating the same request without addressing my concerns. I refuse to expose my family to any further danger. Please tell Seif that I ask him kindly to limit the damage done and tell us the truth.'

'I will.'

*

I heard nothing back for several months. Then, on the evening of the 16th of June, five months after my initial meeting with Seif, Cousin Hamed, Uncle Mahmoud's son, called.

'I have a message for you from my father. "Conditions are worse than we have ever known them to be. We have to pay for water. Prison guards treat us like animals. The food is uneatable. You have a week. If conditions don't improve we will start our hunger strike."'

I could not sleep. As soon as the morning came, I telephoned Seif. There was no answer. I contacted Amnesty International and Human Rights Watch, asking if there was anything they could do. I tried calling Seif again. I then telephoned al-Hawni, who picked up. He sounded sympathetic, said he would speak to Seif. I dialled Seif's number one more time, left him a voice message and then sent him a text version of the same message:

'Relatives in Abu Salim are not well. They are threatening to go on hunger strike.' It was a couple of days later when, sometime past midnight, I got the following text from Seif:

'Today is my birthday ☺'

*

Two days later he texted again:

'Please can you call me 2morrow we need 2 talk.'

I did and he said, 'Your relatives will be moved to another prison to arrange for their release. And, regarding your father, I will draw you a road map. More needs to happen. You need to trust me. There is nothing in it for me. I will lose more than I gain. If you were me, you wouldn't touch it.'

'Men are their actions,' I said.

'Trust me.'

A few minutes later I got this text:

'Most important, don't do anything you don't want. MOSHE DAYAN'

I texted back:

'Be the change you want to see in the world. MAHATMA GANDHI'

He replied:

';->)'

*

Some weeks later, having heard nothing, I called him.

'I don't think you are taking this seriously,' I said. 'You speak of trust but you haven't told me what you know.'

He began screaming down the phone. 'This is complicated; so many are involved, the Mukhabarat, the Egyptians ...'

I interrupted: 'Seif, Seif,' I said.

'What?' he barked.

'There's a problem with the line, you'll have to call me back,' and I immediately hung up.

He called straight away. He repeated what he said but in a much calmer voice. It worked.

'You have it the wrong way round,' I said. 'I don't need anything from you. There is nothing you have that can add or take away anything from me. My father is a crown on my head. What I am offering you is a chance to limit the damage caused. And you wouldn't be doing it for me but for yourself, for history. History will judge. So from now on stop asking me to go out on a limb. I will not take another step before you provide me with what you know.'

*

He telephoned a couple of days later at midnight. He sounded cheerful, friendly. He said he had asked the British to write directly to the Libyan Foreign Ministry requesting information on my father.

'Could you ask the FCO to do it ASAP? As soon as

they issue the letter, I will be able to fulfil on my promise. It will be a headache,' he said. Then, without any irony, he added, 'I'll do it for free.'

*

I contacted the Foreign Office, and a couple of days later I was sitting with Declan Byrne, the FCO's Libya desk officer, and his colleague Philippa Saunders. They told me that the minister for the Middle East, Alistair Burt, had recently met with the Libyan foreign minister, Abdul Ati al-Obeidi. Declan had been present at the meeting. When asked about Jaballa Matar, the Libyan foreign minister had noted the question but said nothing.

They informed me that the letter requested by Seif had been sent that very same day by the prime minister's office to the Libyan embassy.

They then began to speak freely. Declan described the relationship of the British government with Libya as that of 'leveraged engagement'.

'Which, in the Libyan context,' Philippa Saunders said, 'means carrots and nearly no sticks.'

The phrase 'leveraged engagement' reminded me of what Margaret Thatcher used to say in defence of her friendly relations with the South African apartheid regime: 'constructive engagement'.

'And what precisely are you leveraging?' I asked.

They looked at each other, then Philippa said, 'It isn't what you think. It's counterintuitive. Not trade, expertise, education, but Prime Minister David Cameron visiting

Libya for the African Conference. But what Qaddafi wants most from Britain,' she said, blushing slightly, 'is to be taken in a gold carriage down Pall Mall. He has several times requested to meet the queen.'

'But in general,' Declan put in, 'what Libya wants from Britain is international acceptability.'

I asked why they thought Seif seemed willing to help.

'To be seen as the reformer,' Declan said. I couldn't help detect boredom in his voice.

'Out of all the sons,' Philippa Saunders said, 'he is the one that has very little inside Libya. His main credentials are with the West. He is always trying to overcome the gap by proving himself to be the better of the lot, the reformer and progressive. This is a good chance for him, especially in that it relates to Abu Salim and therefore will be seen as a step forward from that dark chapter.'

'Do you believe my father met his end in that massacre?' I asked.

'We don't have any information on that,' Philippa said. 'Frankly, I don't even know if Seif or anyone else in Libya knows.'

*

As soon as I left the Foreign Office, I called Seif.

'The letter you requested reached the Libyan embassy in London today,' I said.

'OK, excellent, excellent,' he said.

That was in August 2010. I had no contact with him or his aides until the 27th of January the following year. Only

a few days earlier, Tunisia had altered the political landscape, as well as the landscape of the imagination,
changing what we could expect of the future and of ourselves. This was happening 700 kilometres west of Tripoli.
Thousands of Tunisians gathered in the Avenue Habib
Bourguiba, the main thoroughfare in the Tunisian capital,
pulsing with songs and demands for democracy. They
succeeded in peacefully ousting a 23-year dictatorship.
Egyptian activists were also mobilizing. Two days before
Seif's call, Cairo's Tahrir Square was filled with demonstrators. Libya's two neighbours had risen. Something
irreversible had begun.

'There was a copy of *The New Yorker* magazine on the
plane,' Seif said when I answered. 'I saw you have a story in it.'

'Did you read it?' I asked.

'It was a short flight. Listen, the file I promised is now
ready and will be delivered to you by Sheik Sulabi. Do you
know him?'

'No.'

'Sheik Sulabi,' he repeated, as though that alone would
tell me more. 'You really don't know him?'

'Never heard of him.'

'He will contact you. I gave him everything.'

'When?'

'Soon, soon,' he said.

'Tell me now,' I said.

'Wait for Sulabi.'

I asked him about my imprisoned relatives.

'I'm fighting a battle, and I will keep on the fight.' He
said the release order had been issued by the prosecutor

but then vetoed 'by someone high up. But I'm doing all I can. It will be resolved soon.'

*

Six days later he telephoned at midnight.

'Have you heard the news?' he said.

'No, what?'

'The release of your relatives – it's done.'

'Are they home?'

'Either tonight or tomorrow. But it's done.'

'That's wonderful,' I said. 'Thank you.'

'And your house too. I have started on it. I spoke to the people who took it and told them off. It will be resolved soon. I've done all this for nothing. It's my moral duty. I only ask that you pray for me, wish me well.'

'It's a testament to your character,' I said. Then I asked him what he made of what was taking place in Egypt.

'It's good,' he said. 'About time. People no longer can do without their freedom.'

*

Eighteen days later, on the 20th of February, Seif appeared on television from Tripoli. Behind him was a map of the world, so large that his bald head barely managed to fill South Africa. He sat slouched in his chair. The tiny island known as the French Southern and Antarctic Lands was a sizeable fleck beside his left shoulder. The South Georgia and the South Sandwich Islands pointed at his right elbow.

He was lost in the Southern Ocean. Below him a banner read: THE SPEECH OF THE ENINEER: SEIF EL-ISLAM MUAMMAR QADDAFI. The misspelling remained until several minutes later, when it was corrected: ENGINEER.

He blamed the uprising on Libyans abroad.

'There are times that demand me to be completely honest. We know that several opposition elements live abroad. What can you say? There are Libyans who oppose us. They have friends and associates and aides and people aligned to them inside the country. They wanted to mimic what happened in Egypt.'

Every so often, he would make a slight movement with his hips, as if his trousers were too tight, then he would pull at his jacket lapels. The long pauses between his repeated statements were so extended it began to seem as if he were hearing voices: that of his father, with whom he had met just before the speech, and perhaps the voices of those who had once believed in him. In different ways, he repeated the same claim: Libyans abroad were conspiring against the country. Everything he said was repeated countless times. The contents of his speech, which lasted thirty-eight minutes, could have been communicated in three minutes. It seemed an appropriate articulation of his father's reign.

The most interesting part of the speech was when he began to offer his predictions. If people did not do as he said, he threatened with unnerving accuracy, a nightmare would follow: civil war, destruction and mass emigration. The carnage he promised proved correct but not for the reasons that might seem obvious. He knew, perhaps more than most, that the system his father built over forty-two years was based on the flimsy premise of 'There is no other option.' But the people had spoken. They ripped open that false barrier. Those who would later lament Seif and his father's regime are like a man who looks at the ashes and says, 'I much prefer the fire.' The calamity that followed the fall of Qaddafi is more true to the nature of his dictatorship than to the ideals of the revolution. All the slogans that were hammered into our ears, which, as children, we were forced to repeat at school, had formed our education. 'A house belongs to whoever lives in it,' which legalized the theft of private property, had indoctrinated in many of us a disregard of the law. 'The masses rule. Representative politics is not democracy. True democracy is by mass rule and the masses must be armed.' These were the slogans that bombarded us from 1969 till 2011. When, in 2009, Larry King asked Seif el-Islam's father, 'What is your proudest achievement?', Qaddafi responded, 'The emergence of the people's authority.'

Watching Seif's speech was like witnessing someone tearing off a mask. He neither apologized nor offered condolences to the families of the demonstrators recently killed by the authorities.

'Instead of crying over eighty-four deaths,' he said, with contempt, wagging his finger at the camera, 'you will be crying over hundreds of thousands of deaths. There will be rivers of blood.' He spoke of Libya as if it were his family's private property. 'This country belongs to us.'

After the speech, he joined his father's savage campaign to crush the dissent. A few days later, Seif's aide, al-Hawni, called from Rome.

'Did you watch the speech?' he asked.

'Yes. Did you write it?'

'Of course not. I am so disappointed.'

'What became of Mohammed Ismail?' I asked.

'The dog. He was at the head of those who attacked the protestors in Benghazi.' Then he said, 'I have written an article about Seif. May I send it to you?'

I was too curious to say no. He called later that afternoon, wanting to know what I thought of it.

'Notwithstanding the convenient timing, it is good that you have finally declared your position. But, to be honest, the article is sentimental and indulges too much in your personal disappointment. You take no responsibility.'

'He was like a son to me. I believed him.'

'But these things are structural. And you were one of those who helped him construct his theatre. He represents a dictatorship, and you have always known that. What is needed now is not this sort of lament but something honest. You need to take responsibility for your misjudgement. For example, where did you think the money came from?'

'What money?'

'The money he was using to fly you around in private jets. The money he bought all that property with.'

'Seif never took a penny from the Libyan people. And if he did, I never knew of it,' Mohammad al-Hawni said.

'But, don't you see, this is exactly the problem. You cannot expect me to believe this. You cannot lick from the honeypot, then pretend you didn't know it was stolen. And do you really expect me to believe that you knew nothing about the Libyan Investment Authority and how Seif used it to bankroll his lifestyle?'

'I didn't know any of this,' he said. He said this in an ingenuous tone, at once disillusioned and disillusioning, betraying an astonishing ability for both sincerity and deception. 'I have always thought Seif's money came from his business. He had a fisheries company in Norway.'

'A fisheries company in Norway,' I said. 'Of course.' I could barely contain my rage. 'It is such deception that needs to be exposed. If you care about Libya, it is this that is worse than the crimes, the murders and the disappearances. This, this … barrage of endless lies. It stinks. Enough.' Struggling to keep the fire at bay, I took a deep breath. 'Listen, listen,' I said, even though he was no longer speaking, 'it's your business what you do and what you write. What I want to know is one thing and one thing only. Now that history has moved on, will you finally tell me what happened to my father?'

'I don't know anything.'

*

A few weeks later, when the cells at Abu Salim prison were hammered open and the blind man in solitary confinement was found with a photograph of my father, Mohammad al-Hawni telephoned again.

'Did you hear that they found a blind man in a cell in the basement? He had a photograph of your father. Do you think, perhaps, I mean, he might be your father, no?'

I hung up.

20. Years

I discovered that the man who had telephoned me back in 2009 to tell me that he had seen my father inside the Mouth of Hell in 2002 was now living in Benghazi. I contacted him and we arranged to meet. We immediately shared our amusement at the fact that, as though by magic, there we were speaking in the open, without fear of being overheard, in a café in Libya. We smoked and talked like surveyors measuring the distance between two fixed points: the time when we spoke over the telephone in 2009, and the present, March 2012, burning brightly, as it seemed then, with hope for the future. And the fact that we were now not disembodied voices over the telephone but flesh and blood, sitting across a table from one another, where it was possible for him to reach across and squeeze my shoulder and for me to do the same in a warm exchange of that victorious camaraderie many of us felt during those hopeful days, seemed to be yet another confirmation of the advantages the present had over the dark past. The present was physical and real; the past, Qaddafi's Libya, was the nightmare from which we had finally awoken.

I wanted to hear more about his encounter with Father, yet at the same time I darkly relished the option of not talking about it. It was somewhere between those two thoughts that I offered, as though we were old friends, to show him a photograph of my father I had stored on my mobile phone.

'Yes, yes,' he said, taking off his glasses, leaning forward. His face, hovering close to the screen, became rigid and vacant.

'This is Jaballa Matar?' he asked.

It was a question – I was sure it was a question – but in the silence that followed I wondered if instead it was more a statement, as in, 'So, this is Jaballa Matar.' The other thought that came to mind was that Father had changed so drastically that this witness was now experiencing the horror I had always feared, the horror of not being able to recognize my father, but experiencing it in reverse, thinking to himself, 'My God, how the man has changed.'

'But this is not Jaballa Matar,' he finally said, leaning back in his chair.

'But, look, this is from many years before,' I said.

'This is not what he looked like,' the man insisted.

I handed him the phone so that he could inspect the picture more closely. He took it in his hand.

'This is from the 1980s,' I explained. 'Some twenty years before you saw him.'

'No,' he said, shaking his head, handing me back the phone. 'This is not the man I saw.'

'What do you mean?' My words came out louder than intended.

I made him nervous.

'There must have been a mistake,' he said. 'You see …
I don't know …'

I must not make him nervous if I am to get the facts, I told myself; to get the facts I must keep him relaxed. I waved to the waiter and asked for a cold bottle of water, two glasses and two more espressos. I handed him a cigarette. We waited in silence until the drinks arrived. The pause transformed him.

'Anyway,' he said, a hint of impatience now in his voice, 'it wasn't me who recognized him. I had no way of recognizing your father. It was one of the other prisoners. He pointed at an old man. "See him there?" he said. "That's Jaballa Matar." That's why when I came out I went around asking for your number. I thought I was doing something good.'

'And I am grateful,' I said. 'The risk you took.'

Instead of parting then and there, I went on trying to change the subject, trying to engage him in small talk, which, at the best of times, I am no good at. But the desire to put him at ease was overwhelming. I was ashamed. There is shame in not knowing where your father is, shame in not being able to stop searching for him, and shame also in wanting to stop searching for him. I continued babbling on, even though every few seconds the muscles in my throat rippled, swallowing, as though a mouthful I had just eaten was now trying to make its way back up my oesophagus. Finally we stood up to say goodbye.

'I am sure you'll find him,' he said with peculiar optimism. 'Nothing remains hidden forever.'

What nonsense, I wanted to say. What complete fucking nonsense. But instead I said, 'Of course.'

*

I remained in the café for a few minutes after he left. Then I wandered out on to the street. It was night, and it felt good that it was night. That man had been the only one who had seen Father alive after the prison massacre of 1996. All the consequences that built on that – the Human Rights Watch report, the campaign, the negotiations with Seif el-Islam – seemed vacuous, a cruel joke. A great wave of exhaustion passed through me. I wished I could cry. I sensed the old dark acknowledgement that Father had been killed in the massacre. I welcomed the feeling. Not only because it was familiar. Not only because certainty was better than hope. But because I have always preferred to think of him dying with others. He would have been good with others. His instinct to comfort and support those around him would have kept him busy. If I strain hard enough, I can hear him tell them, 'Boys, stand straight. With hardship comes ease. With hardship comes ease.' Those other options of him dying alone – those terrify me.

I didn't want to walk by the water. I didn't want to stroll. I wanted the busy downtown, I wanted noise and movement. I found myself by the courthouse, where the lawyers and judges had gathered on the 15th of February 2011. Inside, it had become a shrine to the fallen. The corridors, those same halls where Marwan, Nafa and I used to play as children, waiting for their father, Sidi Ahmed, the High Court judge of Benghazi, to be done for the day, were lined with Photoshopped posters of young men who had died in the revolution. Most showed several images taken from different periods of the deceased's life. They showed him as a toddler, a schoolboy in uniform, at university, at war and dead. They were montaged in a sequence, with the man's name printed across, prefixed by the word MARTYR. This was a new development. The custom in Libya up to then was not to display photographs of the dead until one year had passed after the burial. It was thought the photographs would either interfere with the memory of the bereaved or else excite it too painfully. But now images of these recently deceased young fighters were everywhere. Some families went as far as hiring advertisement hoardings. It was as if the violence had awakened a forgotten ancient tradition. Like pictures of saints, the images of these young men had replaced those of the dictator. Where the various stern and smiling faces of Qaddafi had been, we now had martyrs.

In a large room down one of the long corridors there was a peculiar atmosphere, the sort of silence that is possible only in the presence of others. But the room was empty. Its four walls were clad not in graphically designed posters but in passport-type photographs taken years before, each blown up to the size of a standard letter. Judging from the hairstyles, the original photographs were from the 1960s, '70s and '80s. A scaled architectural model of Abu Salim prison occupied a table in the centre. The room was a memorial to the 1,270 victims of the massacre, the incident that all those years ago had started a chain of events that ultimately led to the overthrow of Qaddafi. I immediately wanted to leave but felt what I had felt on first entering the room, the sensation of having been gripped by something. Even though I was alone, I pretended to be interested or to have the interest of an impartial observer. I tried to look at the faces of the men, but my eyes could not focus. Perhaps, I thought, I will find my father. Perhaps someone knows more than I know and placed his picture here. Perhaps I will find him and be able to enquire and get a piece of paper, a document, stating that Jaballa Matar was one of the 1,270 who perished on the 29th of June 1996, when I was twenty-five, the morning I was for some unremembered reason unable to get out of bed, full of self-pity and regret that, the evening before, I had confided in a friend my money troubles, then walked the fifteen minutes or so that separated my flat from the National Gallery, because I had decided, also for an unknown reason, to leave *The Toilet of Venus*, the goddess of love, by Velázquez, a painting that had awakened in me such sexual desire, and wander over to Manet's unfinished painting, *The Execution of Maximilian*, at about the same hour as the executioners and prison guards in Tripoli were digging the mass grave, rolling the bodies that belonged to these young faces on the walls, one over the next, until the earth was full. Tears, the tears I almost never cry and which had been building up for so long that their place was no longer in the eyes so much as in the belly, began threatening to come up. I couldn't breathe. The faces stared at me. I scanned the rows, searching for Father. It was then that I noticed a woman sitting at a desk in the corner. She had been there the whole time. She was looking at me. I knew that expression. I had seen it before on campaigners. Sympathetic, consoling, dogged. I saw it on volunteers in London, Paris, the Hague, Stockholm, who wrote even more letters than I did, sending one every week to the Libyan government and doing so for ten, fifteen, twenty years, enquiring about my father's whereabouts. They signed petitions and pressured their local representatives. I recognized in this woman now the same unwanted sympathy, the same exercised will. And I recognized in myself the same solidarity, sense of brotherhood and unease I have felt towards such individuals. I still get postcards. The Dutch chapter of Amnesty International had informed their members of my address. Although the address is slightly incorrect, the postman knows by now where to deliver them. They all contain the exact same message, 'Hisham, we support your campaign for truth and justice for your father. We hope you will succeed,' handwritten by children and adults on the back of postcards showing scenic views, a photograph of daffodils printed on a home printer, a child's drawing of hearts with glitter sprinkled on, which sticks to your fingers and comes off only after a couple of washes, a watercolour of the Alps, an earnest white page with the careful, shaky handwriting of the elderly. Poor children, poor people, having to spend afternoons writing such postcards. I never know what to do with them. I put them in a drawer and then throw them away and feel guilty. The woman in the room inspired the same agitated feeling in me.

'You know somebody?' she asked in that slightly pitying tone.

'My father,' I said. 'But he's not here.'

'These,' she said, looking at the photographs, 'are only some of the victims. The aim is to have a complete record.' When I didn't say anything, she added, 'One day.'

'Yes,' I said.

'What is your father's name?' she said.

'Jaballa Matar,' I said.

'Jaballa Matar,' she said, looking at the neatly arranged pieces of paper on the desk in front of her. 'Sounds familiar. Jaballa ... Matar ...' She traced her finger down the list.

It's possible, I told myself; it's possible.

'He doesn't appear to be on the record,' she said. 'These are the confirmed victims, you see. There are many others of course who are not yet confirmed. I know because my nephew died in the massacre.'

'I am sorry,' I said. I had obviously misread her completely. 'I am truly sorry.'

'Me too,' she said.

The tears started pushing up again. Silence, deep breaths – those help. But nothing is more effective than sheer suspicion of the desire to cry. Suspicion almost always keeps me in the clear.

'Have you found any news?' she said.

'No.'

'Are you sure he died in the massacre?'

'No.'

'I hope you find out one day.'

No one in Libya had ever told me this. No one told me they hoped I would find out, only that I will find out. And something about this made me drop my guard. The tears were here. I took a deep breath but it was too late. I faced away, pretending to be looking at the photographs. I clasped my hands behind my waist. I paced, looking at the gallery of faces as though I were one of those people you see in art exhibitions, moving sideways from one picture to the next with hardly a pause, covering up to fifty paintings in an hour, as if the point were to have looked rather than to look. I felt my heart contract and grow small. Pain shrinks the heart. This, I believe, is part of the intention. You make a man disappear to silence him but also to narrow the minds of those left behind, to pervert their soul and limit their imagination. When Qaddafi took my father, he placed me in a space not much bigger than the cell Father was in. I paced back and forth, anger in one direction, hatred in the other, until I could feel my insides grow small and hard. And, because I was young, and hatred and anger are a young man's emotions, I tricked myself into thinking the transformation was good, that it was akin to progress, a sign of vigour and strength. That was how I spent most of my twenties, until, in the autumn of 2002, twelve years on from when I lost my father, I found myself standing at the edge of the Pont d'Arcole in Paris, staring into the green rushing waters below. The novel I was writing was not going well. I felt overwhelmed by the desire to be swept away. I wanted to descend into the depths and be lost forever, taken. Until I heard the bell toll: *Work and survive.* The following day, work on the novel went slightly better. In the days that followed, I threw myself into it completely, and before I knew it I was back inside the book, my thinking, as well as my hours, organized by it.

*

The first signs that something horrible had occurred inside the walls of Abu Salim did not surface until several years after the massacre. Small scraps of information began to emerge, each incomplete, as if careful not to reveal the whole picture at once. I heard the stories and registered them perhaps the way we all, from within our detailed lives, perceive facts – that is, we do not perceive them at all until they have been repeated countless times and, even then, understand them only partially. So much information is lost that every small loss provokes inexplicable grief. Power must know this. Power must know how fatigued human nature is, and how unready we are to listen, and how willing we are to settle for lies. Power must know that, ultimately, we would rather not know. Power must believe, given how things proceed, that the world was better made for the perpetrator than for those who arrive after the fact, seeking justice or accountability or truth. Power must see such attempts as pathetic, and yet the bereaved, the witness, the investigator and the chronicler cannot but try to make reason of the diabolical mess. Each motivated by his or her own need or idea or obsession, they rush this way and that, like ants after a picnic, attending to the crumbs, and time rolls on, infinitely duplicating the distances, furthering us from the original event, making it less possible with every passing day to account for exactly what happened or to be certain, indeed, that anything happened at all. Yet also, with every folding year, like the line of a step mimicking the one before it, it becomes increasingly difficult to escape, to give up altogether on what has been invested so far, least of all the person swallowed up by the injustice. Eventually, the original loss, the point of departure, the point from which life changed irrevocably, comes to resemble a living presence, having its own force and temperament. Like desire, its vitality is in what it withholds, until attachment and resentment are so closely intertwined that it is difficult at times to distinguish one from the other.

It was in 2001 that we began to hear stories of plain-clothed officials arriving unannounced at homes all across the country. They would ask for the household's Family Book – a legal document listing all the members of a nuclear family, their dates of birth and, if deceased, the date and cause of death. A couple of days later the book would be returned. It seemed to be a routine check, and, when asked, the officials said, 'Yes, everything is in perfect order.' The one thing all the families visited had in common was that they had a father, a husband, or a son in Abu Salim.

Most families did not notice the alteration until several days later. I heard of one family who discovered the change only when, a couple of months later, having taken the book out to register a new-born, they saw that the imprisoned grandfather had been dead for several years. One of the stories told is of a woman who looked through her Family Book when it was first returned but noticed nothing different. She searched it carefully and was relieved that all was as it should be. It wasn't until a week or so later that, for reasons she could not account for, she woke up in the middle of the night and went to the drawer where the official document was kept. She could see now what her eyes had not been able to see the first time around. A line written in strong blue ink against her son's name read: 'Died 1996 of natural causes.' She was heard screaming. Her family tried to restrain her, but she managed to run out on to the street. Out of all the words she must have screamed that day, the only one that survived the various retellings of the story was 'Years'. She screamed it over and over. She might have been referring to the years she would have to endure without her son, or those in the past, specifically from the year 1996, in which she continued to make the long journey from where she lived in Benghazi to Tripoli, hoping the prison guards would allow her to see her son. In the years before 1996, she had been allowed visits and even permitted to bring her son clothes, vitamins, food, toothpaste, aftershave. But since June 1996 her twelve-hour trips had been in vain. The guards seemed genuinely sorry. Visits had been indefinitely suspended, they told her, and promised to deliver her gifts, and they never neglected to tell her to try again next month. Every month for five years she cooked meals and purchased gifts for a dead son. She wrote him letters in which she pondered what to say and what to leave out. The guards took it all for themselves, throwing away the letters and eating the food, and sold the other items to the inmates, or took them for themselves, or gifted them to friends or to their own children. Perhaps an aftershave or new pyjamas were given to a son on the occasion of his birthday. 'Years'. That was probably what she meant.

Soon after this, from 2001 onwards, mothers and wives began to camp outside Abu Salim prison, holding framed photographs of their sons and husbands. Their grief was never acknowledged. They kept growing in number, until the moment when a young human rights lawyer decided to defy the wishes of the dictatorship and take up the case of the families. When in 2011 he was detained, they all marched to the Benghazi courthouse to demonstrate against his arrest.

*

I spent the rest of the evening walking with Diana through the city. I like watching her photograph. The stillness of concentrated effort. But I have never liked the attention it attracts. Although people here in Benghazi were relaxed. This too would soon change. Journalists, Libyan and foreign, were going to be prime targets for kidnapping and assassination; as a consequence, events in the country would go largely unreported, and the only way anyone could hope to learn of what was going on would be through social-media websites.

Diana went into a square off Omar al-Mukhtar Street. At the centre there was a large tiled rectangular area with benches and a few palm trees. It was surrounded on all four sides by low-rise blocks of flats. Something about the square appealed to her. She is not one to photograph a pretty sunset. She is after something else. She set up her tripod in the middle of the square, and pointed the large box camera towards one corner. She often photographs at night, and never uses flash or spotlights. She measured the lux level in order to determine how long the shutter would need to remain open. She clicked, keeping her finger on the button for two whole minutes. To be sure, she took two more shots: one at one minute and a half and another at three minutes. During this time I sat on one of the benches. The soft sounds of the lives of families – cutlery, television, chatter – floated out of the windows of the surrounding flats. Around one of the benches a group of young men gathered. They were smoking. I could smell the sweet stink of hashish. Suddenly two young boys – they couldn't have been more than ten – ran into the square and stood facing one another. Other boys their age circled around them. They were in all the Libyan skin colours: black, brown and white. A couple of the men smoking sauntered over and separated the boys before a fight could begin. There was something oddly predictable about it all, as though it were part of a pre-planned performance. The young boys scattered off in different directions.

Once Diana was done, I helped her pack up and we left the square. We did not notice that we were being followed. We were already walking up Omar al-Mukhtar Street when a young boy called after us.

'Ustath, ustath.' He looked shy. 'Are you journalists?' he asked. He was one of the boys who had nearly come to blows. He had an unforgettable face, tender and bright. Standing beside him was another boy, who looked as if he were there to offer support.

'No,' I said. 'Not journalists. My wife is an artist and I'm a writer.'

'Are you part of those who came earlier asking about the families of the disappeared?'

'No, why? Do you know one of the disappeared?'

'My brother.'

'How old is he?'

'Twenty-five. He was arrested at a demonstration on the 25th of March 2011.'

'I'm sorry,' I said. 'I hope you find him soon.'

'Thank you.'

'It's awful, isn't it?'

He nodded.

'It's hard to know what to do.'

He looked away. I thought I must say something positive.

'But have faith, and make sure you attend to your studies.'

He nodded again.

'My father too disappeared,' I said.

'May God bring him back safely,' he said. Then, after a pause, he asked, 'When did it happen?'

'Many years ago. On the 12th of March 1990.'

He looked at me and then looked away again.

I translated for Diana, then told the boy what she said. 'My wife says she hopes you find your brother very soon.'

'Where's she from?' his friend beside him, who was even smaller, asked.

The other boy looked at him as if to say, 'Don't be rude.'

'America,' I said.

'America?' the friend said.

I asked him if he too knew someone who had disappeared.

'No,' he said, thrusting his little fists out against the fabric of his T-shirt.

'I'm glad,' I said. Then, when neither of them spoke, I said, 'OK, then, goodbye.'

'Where are you staying?' the boy said.

I gave him the name of the hotel.

He thought a little, then asked, 'The one on the water?'

'Exactly,' I said.

'OK. Good night,' he said.

We walked away. When I looked back, I found them still standing in the same spot. I waved but they didn't wave back. Several times on the way to the hotel, Diana and I thought of returning and finding some excuse to spend more time with them. The feeling persisted till the following day. We went back to the square and spent about an hour there, but the boys never turned up.

21. The Bones

In these days spent in Benghazi, I often detected a strange attachment to Ajdabiya. I never had it as a child. It has been growing through the years, snatching away my longing from Tripoli, where we lived and I spent my childhood, away from Benghazi, where my brother and I spent summers with cousins, and taking it to Ajdabiya, that austere and earnest town I was never fond of as a boy. If my father had been alive, he would have been seventy-three. When I used to imagine being reunited with him, I had always pictured it happening not in our home in Cairo, the place from which he was taken, not in London, where I lived and I wondered at times, given Egypt's betrayal, if he might choose to live after his release, but in my grandfather's house in Ajdabiya. It was as though I were returning him, in my imagination, to his father's house. I imagined it taking place not in secret, not in the night hours, as when he made those perilous visits, sneaking across the Egyptian–Libyan border in order to visit Grandfather Hamed, but in a day full of light.

*

I returned to Ajdabiya. This time I went alone.

Uncle Hmad Khanfore had been away on my first visit.

I had campaigned for his release for years, but we had never met before. He loved the theatre, Mother had told me, and when in the old days he visited my parents in Cairo, she took him to at least three plays a week. There is a photograph of him with Mother and Cousin Ali, all sitting in a row on one of the decorated horse-drawn carriages by the Nile. Even the driver is smiling towards the camera, holding his long whip upright beside him. A few months after this photograph was taken, Uncle Hmad and Ali were arrested. I looked at the photograph several times during their twenty-one years of incarceration: Uncle Hmad, who had plans of becoming a playwright, and Cousin Ali, who had just returned from studying economics at the University of Düsseldorf and had about him, in the way he dressed and sat upright, a curious Germanic formality. The next photograph I saw of them was taken on the day of their release and emailed to me the following day. It shows uncles Mahmoud and Hmad and cousins Ali and Saleh standing in front of the prison gate. They are wearing clean, ironed clothes. Each man is two decades older. Not only the hair but the skin too seems to have faded in colour. They are looking towards the camera, trying to smile, trying to seem comfortable. What did you expect, I told myself. Joy? This is no occasion for joy. When you are released from such a long incarceration, the full scale of the injustice takes shape. Only then can you realize how much time has passed, how much the world has changed, and how much has been lost. But even then I somehow knew it wasn't only that. Something was off.

I had met Cousin Ali in Cairo just before I flew to

Benghazi. He was on a brief visit. I gave him directions over the phone and stood at the corner of the street, waiting. I felt such excitement at the prospect of finally meeting him. When he drove in I could see that, just like me, he could not stop from smiling. He parked and we embraced. This is the body that has been locked away for two decades. This is the body that belongs to the name I repeated in my letters to various governments and NGOs. We sat side by side on the sofa and chatted until lunch was served. He said many things about life in prison, but what stayed with me most was his description of the loudspeakers. Father had mentioned them in one of his prison letters. But it was far worse than I had imagined. The speakers were not in the corridors but inside each cell, fixed to the high ceiling, where they could not be reached or torn off. They played speeches by Qaddafi, interrupted only by propaganda songs and slogans expounding the virtues of the regime. The broadcast was on every day from 6 a.m. to midnight, and at full volume.

'So loud,' Ali said, 'that it was hard sometimes to make out the words. You could feel your muscles vibrate. I used to lie down and watch the small empty plastic bottle tremble on the concrete floor.' Then, perhaps to console me, he added, 'But you got used to it eventually.' Suddenly he said, 'I want to thank you.'

'What for?' I asked.

'For everything you did.'

The tone in which he said this was complicated. It was sincere and reticent, both appreciative and regretful. It corresponded with that photograph taken on the day of their release.

Later that afternoon, Ali disclosed a new piece of information. After Seif's aides had informed him and the others of their release, that they were finally going home, after telling them that 'tonight you'll sleep in your beds', after providing them with clean clothes, razors and shaving cream, after giving them a chance to say farewell to the other prisoners, after walking them across the courtyard and into an office furnished with large sofas and several armchairs, after they served them tea and coffee and handed them cigarettes, all done with an air of jovial courtesy and ease, they were told that their release was contingent on one final detail: 'Signing a formal apology for having ever opposed the Great Leader.' Seif had already prepared it. Someone had typed it up and it was there, with a dotted line beside each man's name. All must sign or none could be released.

'I didn't want to do it,' Ali told me. 'But Mahmoud had reached the end of his tether. He was ill and frail. I was worried about him.'

To have to sign an apology after twenty-one years of cruel and unjust imprisonment can break a man. Had I done nothing, they would have walked out anyway when the revolutionaries took over Abu Salim and hammered open the doors. But I acted on the facts I had then. Seif never mentioned an apology, and, even if he had, it would have been inappropriate for me to deny my uncles and cousins the choice. Nonetheless, this new piece of knowledge corrupted everything, and from then on, whenever

anyone thanked or congratulated me on the role I had
played in the release of my uncles and cousins, I quickly
changed the subject.

*

Uncle Hmad seemed oddly young and old at once, as if
his younger self, with its love for the theatre and a thousand and one plans for the future, had been restrained and
conserved by captivity. This is not unusual, I suppose; our
younger selves are with us always. But in a life of activity,
one free from dramatic rupture, where the progress of
things is unbroken by catastrophe, where the skin of our
thoughts is regularly touched by new impressions, discoveries and influences, our maturation comes to follow a
gradient that creates the illusion of a seamless line. With
Uncle Hmad, the young man he was at the point of his
arrest and the man he had become seemed to exist in parallel, destined never to meet and yet resonating against
one another like two discordant musical notes.

His English was good and he was keen to speak to me
in it. Part of his consciousness was constantly occupied
with those around him. This exceptional thoughtfulness,
I imagined, must have left him exhausted at the end of
each social engagement. I am nowhere near as thoughtful
yet I find it impossible to be 'myself' in the company of
others. I am constantly thinking about those around me.
If I like them, my opinions sway in their direction, and if
for whatever reason they irritate me, I am wilfully obstin-
ate. Either way, I am left weary and unclear, regretting

ever having relinquished my solitude, and, because I desire the company of others and always have, the cycle is endless. Perhaps, I thought, Uncle Hmad suffered from the same affliction. This was one of the reasons I felt an immediate sympathy towards him. I wanted to listen to him, and he, in turn, was eager to share his recollections. Perhaps we both suspected then that our time together was going to be limited, that the world was going to change and the routine of frequent trips to Libya, or possibly even living there for part of the year, was no longer going to remain an option.

'Technically speaking,' Uncle Hmad said, talking in English, 'Uncle Jaballa was my brother-in-law, but I regarded him as a father, and not only because of the age difference. He was a role model,' he added and looked at me with those eyes I had seen before on men who love my father. From then on, I dropped the 'Uncle' and referred to him simply as Hmad.

*

These encounters with my relatives who had spent decades in prison, whose names have been on my tongue and between my fingers repeatedly over the many years I campaigned and wrote letters about them to various governments and human rights organizations, exposed the riptides between us. They wanted to tell me about what life was like during the two decades in prison, and I was keen to let them know how much I thought of them. It was an exchange of promises and devotion, one coloured, on their part, by the excitement of those who have survived an accident, and, on mine, by the guilt of having lived a free life – guilt but also a stubborn shamelessness that, yes, I had lived a free life. In other words, our company provoked an assault of judgements inflicted by the self and therefore always possibly imagined. They wanted me to know that their loyalty to Father had not faltered, and I wanted them to know that I had not neglected them but done all I could. They wanted me to know how they felt about my father, and, in doing so, I felt, they were acknowledging what they refused to accept: that he was dead. They had more things to tell me than I had to tell them. They wanted to bring me into the darkness, to expose the suffering and, in doing so, discreetly and indirectly emphasize the bitter and momentous achievement of having survived it. Is there an achievement greater than surviving suffering? Of coming through mostly intact? And I sensed enjoyment in their telling, in having the savage horror of their time in prison – a period covering between one-third to one-half of each man's life so far – sit side by side with the gentleness of a liberal afternoon with tea and cigarettes.

'I will die for his right to speak his mind,' I heard Uncle Mahmoud say. Then he cut someone off to call out to me, 'Isn't that right, Ibn Jaballa? Do you know that line? Voltaire, isn't it?' and he repeated it with relish.

On my previous visit, in a moment when we were alone, Uncle Mahmoud had told me how he'd had everything done to him. 'They beat me, deprived me of food and sleep, tied me down, spilled a bucketful of cockroaches on my chest. There is nothing they didn't do. Nothing can happen to me now that can be worse than that time. And always, I managed it. I kept a place in my mind, where I was still able to love and forgive everyone,' he said, his eyes soft and lips smiling. 'They never succeeded in taking that from me.'

*

Hmad and I sat on the floor in one corner of Uncle Mahmoud's living room. We talked in soft voices so as not to disturb the other half of the room, now engaged in a conversation focusing on the current situation: the lack of security and the proliferation of arms.

'Who on earth will collect all these weapons?' one asked.

'There are guns in every house across the country,' another said.

Hmad began talking of the massacre. I assumed he wanted to start there because it was this event that sparked the blaze. Like the beginnings of those fires that eat up entire forests, the 2011 revolution too had had a specific beginning, one to marvel at, we then felt. But I suspected Hmad started there also because it was after the Abu Salim massacre that my father was never seen again. Did Hmad believe Father died in the massacre? Exactly at the moment I thought I dared not ask, I heard myself say, 'Was Father killed there?'

'Only God knows,' Hmad said.

'I know,' I said, checking that my voice was soft, as if

we were talking about the waters this time of the year. 'But what do you think?'

'Only God knows,' he said again. 'In the early days we could hear and talk to him. He was in a cell not too far away, but then they moved him and we were no longer in contact, except by the occasional letter.'

I needed to change the subject. I asked him about his children, if it was true that now he lived in Grandfather Hamed's old house.

'Yes,' he said, smiling. 'But it's not as you remember it. So much has changed. You must visit.'

'I will,' I said.

'Anyway, my dear man, let me bring it to you from the beginning. Months before the massacre,' Hmad said, resuming his account, 'there was a protest in the prison. The causes were cumulative. Conditions had always been dismal, but mostly stable and predictable, but then, in November 1995, thirteen prisoners escaped. Our treatment deteriorated drastically.

'The most terrible man – I will never forget him – was El Magroos. When he sat on a chair, it was as though he were sitting on a tin of baby milk powder. A stick in his hand looked as small as a toothpick. The man was a giant. And all muscle. When he was done interrogating you, he would begin to taunt you. This was the custom. Not only to ridicule and provoke, but also to kill time. The thing was, these guards and interrogators were terribly bored, always looking for something to amuse them.

'I remember once, after they questioned me for hours, El Magroos asked, "Do you want to go back to your cell?"

'Now, this will be hard for you to believe,' Hmad said, 'but when I was asked this question, it landed on my ear as sweetly as though I were being asked if I wanted to go home. Imagine?' Hmad said, tapping my leg. 'The interrogations were so awful that when they finally took you back to the cell, you were as happy returning to that miserable place as you would be going home to your wife and children. I was finished, exhausted and bleeding from several places.

'"OK, then," El Magroos said. "You can go back to your cell but only after I hear you say that Jaballa Matar is a stray dog."

'"But what good would that do?" I said.

'"I want to hear you say it," he said.

'I told him, "Listen, I would rather speak words that would cut off my head than those that would lower it."

'The other interrogator was moved by this and told him, "Let him go." El Magroos refused.

'"I am no hero," I told him, "but I tell you, you can beat me with that stick for as long as you like; I won't say it. And what good would it do you anyway if I were to say it? Nothing. Whereas for me, it would break me."

'Thankfully the other man intervened again. I was lucky, because if they had beaten me I would have said it – I would have said anything.

'When Mahmoud and the others saw me,' Hmad said, laughing, 'they were baffled. I was black and blue but happy. I could sleep.'

With every vapour in my body I longed to smoke. I offered Hmad a cigarette and we both lit up.

'Anyway, let me return to the events that preceded the massacre,' he said, exhaling. 'Like I told you, the dismal treatment worsened after those men escaped. The few luxuries we had were taken away: soap, pillows, mattresses – till all that remained was the concrete floor. We became as thin as ghosts.

'A few months into this hell, a new group was put in the cell opposite ours. In comparison, our conditions were luxurious. They had staged an armed confrontation in Benghazi, trying to take over a garrison. One of them was a man called Khaled al-Baksheesh. They beat him till they broke his thigh, then left him without treatment or pain-killers. We used to hear him moan. His leg began to rot. One day his cellmates kept banging on the door till the guards came. They took Khaled al-Baksheesh to the courtyard beside our wing. We were relieved, thinking they would take him to hospital. I saw his withered leg. I couldn't believe it. It stretched horribly behind him like a rope. They placed him in the middle of the courtyard and aimed water hoses at him. They kicked him all the way back to his cell. That night we heard nothing. In the morning his cellmates told us he was dead.

'It was this group in the cell opposite – Cell Number 9 – that set off the disobedience. I remember the day well. It was a Friday, Friday, the 28th of June 1996. As soon as the afternoon prayer was over, I heard shouting, a scuffle and gun shots. What had happened was that when the guards opened Cell Number 9 to push in the food, the men jumped the guards. They took their guns and keys and let out all the prisoners. We gathered in the corridor, not really sure what to do next. Guards on the floor above began firing. Some prisoners were killed and others wounded. We hid back in our rooms. We would occasionally risk it and run from one cell to the next. The standoff remained for hours.

'Something strange happened. You are not going to believe it, but I swear to you on my children's life. One of the prisoners killed, his body remained exactly the same, only a little paler in the cheeks, but otherwise unchanged. It smelt of musk. We didn't have musk or such things in the prison. And the face of the prison guard who had been dead the same number of hours was now black and his body bloated like a balloon and stinking horribly. We all marvelled at this.

'By sunset, one of the guards called out, promising water – they had turned off the mains to force us to surrender. He asked us to nominate one man from each wing to negotiate with them. Our representatives went off and were gone a long time. When they returned, they were accompanied by three of the most senior figures in the regime: Abdullah Senussi, who was the intelligence chief and brother-in-law to Qaddafi; Abdullah Mansour, also in intelligence; and Khairi Khaled, the head of prisons and brother of Qaddafi's first wife. Basically, some of the most important people, none more so than Abdullah Senussi, who was very cordial.

'"What's the problem, my brothers?" he asked. "Why are you so upset?"

'We told him our treatment was unbearable and that we preferred to die than live like this. "Human rights –

what human rights?" we told him. "We don't even have animal rights. At least animals are fed and watered and not beaten. We get none of these privileges and our ill are left to die."

"'These are all your demands?" Abdullah Senussi asked. "In that case, these are very reasonable demands," he said. "I don't even need to consult anyone. I will implement your requirements right away. Consider all of your grievances to be behind you now."

'Throughout these exchanges, Senussi was in regular contact with Qaddafi. His phone would ring and he would stand as straight as a reed and start whispering. His phone rang again now, and once more we watched him take a couple of steps away before answering, "Yes, Your Excellency. The situation is completely under control, Your Excellency. Absolutely, we will do exactly that. Rest assured." He hung up and asked us all to go back to our cells. "When you wake up," he told us, "you will find everything has changed."

'We asked for senior figures from the legal community as well as foreign ambassadors to witness the agreement.

"'We are the government and you are the prisoners," Senussi said. "If we want, we can tonight send fighter jets to bomb the entire prison with you and the guards in it. We neither fear you nor feel for you. But we decided, out of humility and kindness, to reason with you," he said. A few minutes later he called out, "Listen, to reassure you of our good intentions, give us 120 men, those most in need of medical care, and I will personally, with my own hand, deliver them to the Salah el-Din hospital."

'This final promise,' Hmad told me, 'was a huge temptation. Arguments ensued amongst us.

'"In the meantime, as you are trying to make up your minds," Senussi shouted across the corridor, "gather up the ill and wounded. We will even take the dead and bury them. Tomorrow I promise you a new set of guards, respectable food and respectable treatment. You will think you woke up in a five-star hotel," he said.

'The prisoners argued. There was real tension now. Several called out, "Come on, let's assume the best. Select 120. Thirty men from each wing."

'From our wing the thirty men included my brother Ahmed, your cousins Ali and Saleh, a couple of others from Uncle Jaballa's group, your uncle Mahmoud and me. None of us slept that night.

'At dawn, before daybreak, when the sky was still completely black, we were marched into the big open yard. I couldn't believe what I saw. Rows and rows of soldiers, all dressed for battle, several of them poised in firing positions. They numbered so many that it seemed the entire Libyan army was gathered there. How did we not hear them arrive, I wondered. The prison guards carried the dead prisoners in wheelbarrows and dumped them in the large rubbish bins. The rest of us were handcuffed with what we called Israeli cuffs. They were manufactured there. The latest design. A thin plastic wire that drew tighter with the slightest resistance. You felt the pain not so much around the wrists but inside the head.

'We were all put on to large buses. I sat by the window. I saw a man, I didn't know who he was, but from the way he was dressed and the way several people followed him around, I knew he was in charge. He entered the bus I was on and called out, "Who amongst you are from the Ajda-biya Group?"

'Ali was on the same bus; so was another man, seated right in front of me. I whispered to him that we should announce ourselves.

"'No," he said.

'The official repeated, "The Ajdabiya Group, the oppo-sition, from the 1990 case: make yourselves known."

'I put my hand up.

"'Who else is with you?" the man asked.

'I pointed to Ali. I didn't mention the other man. I didn't want to be responsible.

'Ali and I came down from the bus and saw Saleh, my brother Ahmed, Mahmoud and a couple of others from our group gathered there too. We were lined up and ordered to go down on our knees. The Israeli cuffs felt as though they were about to slice my hands off. We remained like this till morning broke. Then I heard from behind us the same senior official order one of his subordinates to place our names in our pockets. We were asked to state our names. They wrote each one down, folded the piece of paper and shoved it into our pocket. That's it, I thought, my hour has come. But then there was confusion. They brought everyone down from the buses and packed them all into a sort of barn structure that we called the work-shop. They took our small group back inside and locked us up in a new cell. A few seconds later we heard a loud explosion, then dense and unceasing gunfire – all sorts of weapons: pistols, machine-guns – and the sound of men screaming, all coming from the workshop. It turned out – we learnt this much later from one of the guards who took part in the shooting – that Abdullah Senussi had initiated the massacre by throwing a hand grenade into the workshop. That was the explosion.

'But that was just the beginning. A dark atmosphere and a great energy was cutting through the prison now. Guards were rushing from one cell to the next with lists of names. Hundreds of prisoners were rounded up. They were handcuffed and taken into the courtyards. These spaces were roofless and rectangular, about ten metres by forty-five metres, the surrounding structure being about eight metres high. Six such courtyards were filled. Soldiers and prison guards took their places on the surrounding roof. The shooting began.'

'How did you know this?' I asked. 'Did you see it?'

'No, but it was witnessed by those in the cells that overlooked the courtyards. And, later, some of the guards who were there told us what happened. But I heard it all. The shooting lasted for two hours.'

'I met a man once,' I told Hmad, 'who had described it as a drill inside the head.'

'It was,' he said. 'But worst of all was the screaming. You heard it clearly when the machine-gun fire stopped. Then came the sporadic pistol shots, the coup de grâce, we assumed. The dead were left there for four days. Until the smell caused many of us to vomit.'

My mind would not stop. It flashed images of my father in this diabolical nightmare. I saw part of his foot, then his ankle lying still on the ground, dusted by the movement of others. His creased palm, half closed. The gentle strength of his torso. And, for a quick instant, his face. An expression I couldn't understand. Sadness and exhaustion and an infinite sympathy, as though his sorrow was not only for the fallen but for the perpetrators too. All this together with a final and inconsolable realization that he would never see us again. I felt the violent force of vertigo. As though he and I were standing on opposite sides of a river, and the water was growing wider, as wide as an ocean now.

'Gradually, the guards began to talk,' Hmad said. 'They wanted to talk because they saw everything. They were particularly interested in what happened to us, the Ajdabiya Group, and how we got away. "You were amongst the first," they would say. "How on earth did you manage to survive?" They would laugh about it, as you would about a curiosity.

'Every day I think of that friend who was in the bus in front of me.'

The bodies were buried where they fell, in shallow mass graves. Months later, they were exhumed. The bones were ground to dust and the powder poured into the sea.

22. The Patio

Another round of tea was served and I lit up another cigarette. I was smoking too much. My chest felt fogged up with nicotine. Uncle Mahmoud said something to Hmad about not keeping me all to himself. Hmad smiled. They have an ease with one another. I noticed it too with Saleh. After their initial arrest, they were all put in the same cell. This arrangement, sitting and talking softly in clusters on different sides of the same room, must be familiar to them. I remembered how, on meeting Ali earlier in Cairo, we decided to telephone Uncle Mahmoud to tell him about the happy occasion. I handed the phone to Ali and was taken aback by the harsh tone he employed with his uncle. 'So this is what you're like?' he told him. 'Days pass and you don't even call.' I expected Ali to laugh, as usually happens after such affectionate admonishments, but he kept the stern face, ending the call with, 'I'll see you when I see you, then.' They were so close, I remember thinking, that they could do this, they could be upset at each other and could just leave it at that. When you live together in the same room you can leave it at that, but in a world where anything can happen, and where the distances are forever stretching, we must try to make amends at the very first opportunity. This sort of intimacy, the complicity and dismissal it allows, as though they didn't have to pay attention to one another any more, was rare and curious. It seemed they had no anxiety about losing one another. Perhaps it is the anxiety of losing someone that keeps us attached. But that is a different sort of attachment. This is another, much finer form, I remember thinking.

'There is so much I want to tell you,' Hmad said, smiling.

'And I want to hear it all,' I said.

'Did anyone tell you that I was a poet?' he said.

'No, no one told me.'

'But, unlike these ignorant fools,' he said, loud enough for Uncle Mahmoud and the others to hear, 'I wrote my poems in English.'

'He has always been a foreigner,' Uncle Mahmoud said.

'They only came in English,' Hmad said. 'They used to come in prison. Now I don't remember any.'

'Didn't you write them down?' I asked.

'We weren't allowed to write anything down. I got beautiful letters from your father. I either burnt them or tore them up and flushed them down the toilet as soon as I read them. If you were caught with one, you and the author of the letter would spend a day in hell.'

It was as though I were drowning. Anywhere I go here, I will stumble on my father.

'What did he write you?' I asked.

'There is one letter I remember well. Now, you have to keep in mind that these letters were smuggled through a long and convoluted network of secret passages between the cells, and sometimes they had to be destroyed before they could reach their intended reader.'

'Where did you find paper and pens?'

'There was always a guard who would sell us some and look the other way. At one point Uncle Jaballa fell silent for a long time. We wondered if he was all right. I wrote him, and several weeks later I got a reply. I still remember the line where he said, "Don't worry; I am well. I am like the mountain that is neither altered nor diminished by the passing storms."'

I felt numb and cold – I don't mean indifferent but literally shivering inside and helpless. I remembered silently, for I would have never dared tell Hmad, Father's intimate disclosure in the recorded letter he sent us, how at its end he allowed himself to weep and didn't erase it. There was something desperate about having those two impressions, steadfastness and despair, sit side by side. I felt an abject confinement, as though I were lost in a tunnel. And I remembered once again Telemachus's words:

> I wish at least I had some happy man
> as father, growing old in his own house –
> but unknown death and silence are the fate
> of him ...

And for the first time those familiar words, which have been to me loyal companions for many years, moved and expanded in meaning. They were now just as much about Odysseus as they were about Telemachus; just as much about the father as they were about the son; just as much about the wish of the son to have his father spend the remainder of his days in the comfort and dignity of his own house as they were about the son's wish to finally be able to leave the father at home, to finally turn and face forward and walk into the world. As long as Odysseus is lost, Telemachus cannot leave home. As long as Odysseus is not home, he is everywhere unknown.

*

'Speaking of poems,' Uncle Mahmoud said, 'you must come see this.'

He stood up and I followed him to a cabinet. He pulled open a drawer and took out a folded piece of white linen. It used to be a pillowcase. It was so sheer you could see through it. He spread it out.

'I stole it,' he said, smiling. 'Then I picked out the thread and turned it into a single sheet.'

Both sides of it were covered in writing. It looked like a membrane with intricate patterns. Uncle Mahmoud began to read to me. They were poems and letters he had written over several years to his children. A thin line separated each cluster of text. It resembled a diagram of the human anatomy: one letter in the shape of a kidney, another filling up a lung, a poem doing its best to occupy the gap between.

'These are the only jottings I managed to keep from all those years,' Uncle Mahmoud said. 'They are possibly the only surviving literature from all the countless volumes that have been authored inside Abu Salim prison,' he said, laughing.

He had managed this by folding the fabric into a strip and sewing it to the waistband of his underpants.

*

We ate lunch. I felt exhausted and empty. I must have looked sleepy because Uncle Mahmoud insisted I take a nap in Izzo's room. It was odd lying down on the bed of my dead cousin. There were pictures of him on each wall. I was conscious of the mattress pressing against the length of my body.

When I woke up I went and stood with Aunt Zaynab in the kitchen. It was that afternoon hour I remember so well, when a Libyan house is neither asleep nor fully awake. It is when the entire street, indeed the world, seems vacant. The kitchen door to the patio was open. The sun was strong yet well past its summit. It entered in a skewed triangle, stretching across the kitchen floor, making the rest of the room oddly dull and static, like an abandoned place. Someone, probably Hamed or Amal, had taken a hose to the patio. The water had evaporated but the tiles were still dark with moisture. A cool soft breeze was swirling into the kitchen. Aunt Zaynab looked at me and smiled.

'You want to help?' she asked, kneading dough. Every time she folded it, tiny bubbles of air burst through. 'Hand me that bowl,' she said.

The dish was made of wafer-thin aluminium, hammered into a perfect contour, as if a third of a globe had been sliced off. Its weight was nearly non-existent. She placed it upside down on top of a flame. With the amused pride of a talented cook who knows she is being observed, she worked the dough in her hands, stretching it. She wet a finger and tested the metal. It made a sizzling sound when she touched it. She pulled the dough into a thin sheet and dropped it on to the metal helmet of the bowl.

The dough drew together tightly as soon as it touched the heat and slowly began to rise.

'How was your nap?' she asked.

I chose not to say anything about how odd it was to be in Izzo's room, to have my head on his pillow. Nor did I tell her about how, although I had slept for only about twenty minutes, I had had a powerful dream that seemed to last for hours. It had incorporated a real television interview with a rebel from Benghazi that I had watched immediately after that city was liberated. The man stood out because he was exactly my age, and, amongst the jubilations of that day, he did not seem all that happy. 'I want to publicly apologize,' he started. 'I want to publicly apologize, on behalf of my entire generation, to all the young boys who had to fight. We should have done it for you earlier . . . You needn't have died like this.' In my dream the man had been transformed into Izzo, surrounded by children, some of them laughing and pulling faces at the camera. I said none of this to Aunt Zaynab. Instead, I said, 'I slept well.' Which was true.

'Was the bed comfortable?'

'Very.'

'It's Izzo's bed,' she said.

She kept turning the pastry until it was golden on both sides. The kitchen smelt like warm skin. She handed me the tub of date syrup. I poured some of the thick black liquid into a small white bowl. I could hear the voices of Uncle Mahmoud and his children outside. I filled several glasses with yoghurt milk and carried it all on a tray to the patio.